HOW MUCH IS ENOUGH?

GETTING MORE BY LIVING WITH LESS

An Interactive Memoir by
CLAIRE BERGER

Printed in the United States of America
Paperback ISBN: 978-1-961624-46-7
Ebook ISBN: 978-1-961624-47-4

**Canoe Tree
Press**

Canoe Tree Press is a division of DartFrog Books
301 S. McDowell St.
Suite 125-1625
Charlotte, NC 28204
www.DartFrogBooks.com

Don't make yourself small.
Not for anyone.
If someone tells you
you're too much . . .
too loud, too sensitive,
too fierce, too caring,
too intellectual, too optimistic,
too realistic, too logical, too emotional . . .
just smile and move on, my friend.
Clearly, they aren't enough for you.
—L.R. Knost

You are enough—more than enough. You just have to love and appreci-
ate yourself enough.
—Gift Gugu Mona

In the pursuit of perfection, I forgot I was already enough.
—Caroline George

Table of Contents

These chapters may be read in any order, in any room of your house, on any mode of transportation (except when driving), on your vacation, coffee break, lunch hour, at a sporting event, in a doctor's waiting room, or while waiting for an Internet date who may or may not show up. Read the ones that speak directly to you first.

Introduction

How Much Is Enough, my interactive memoir, is culled from sixty-seven years of a very unpredictable, occasionally glamorous, intermittently tragic, often hilarious life. I wrote this book to start a very personal conversation with you, my inquisitive reader. Whether our conversation takes place in a concert hall, in a cozy window seat nestled under a soft, fuzzy throw, through Zoom, or inside your head, my wish is that this collection of essays serve as kindling for self-reflection and that it inspires impactful contemplation about the concept of *enough* in all aspects of your life.

Since 2020, we've had more than enough time for self-reflection. Time spent in Covid lockdown—alone or in an anxious, intermittently neurotic bubble of family members—certainly gave me pause to do an emotional inventory of sorts. When so much day-to-day normalcy is stripped from my life, what is left to embrace and appreciate? How much is enough time spent worrying about our world's overall health? How many calls to my adult children are enough to be supportive without being clingy? And can I finally stop shaving my legs?

Have you experienced a dramatic shift in your life that has given you pause to reevaluate your own sense of *enough*?

Mid-pandemic, I decided to reinvent my life. I left everything familiar—my home, my steady income, and many people I loved, including my adult son, Sam—and I moved from keto-obsessed Los Angeles to bagel-loving Brooklyn with my daughter, Jenna; my son-in-law, Patrick; my granddaughter, Natalie; and their French bulldog, Bridget. It was a bold move.

After unpacking my drastically pared-down possessions into my new, much smaller New York apartment and learning the local dialect (*Fuggedaboutit!*), one of the first things I did was to join my neighborhood YMCA. It has a beautiful pool, and I looked forward to the chance to enjoy regular exercise. I mustered up the courage to make new friends in my extremely alluring swim cap and goggles ensemble in the socially challenging, pandemic environment. I paid my membership and learned the rules of the pool. It was April 2021, and pandemic protocols were still in place. The number of people in the pool at one time and the length of time anyone could swim were strictly monitored. Each person was assigned a lane and had exactly thirty minutes to swim. When my time was up, I would climb out of the pool and give the next swimmer a chance to dive in.

I made every one of those thirty minutes count. I focused on my strokes, my kicks, my steady speed, and, most importantly, my breathing. My body felt weightless as I swam, and the stretches that each stroke and kick provided gave me relief from intermittent back spasms and other minor aches and pains. I let my mind wander while I stole furtive underwater glances at my fellow Brooklyn swimmers' elaborate tattoos. Before I knew it, my thirty minutes were up, my breathing was heavy, and my heart rate had risen. I exited the pool with a feeling of accomplishment, confident that I had completed a solid workout, both mentally and physically.

Once the Covid numbers began to drop, the Y removed the time limit. Now I could swim longer than thirty minutes if I wanted to, but I had become accustomed to my thirty-minute swim, so I kept doing that. Before the time limit was dropped, I'd felt triumphant after every thirty-minute swim, so why was I now judging myself for swimming for *only* thirty minutes? Day after day, I asked myself that same question: How much swimming is *enough*? Sure, I would burn more calories if I swam more, but could I also be satisfied with just being a thirty-minute swimmer? No one would mistake me for seven-time Olympic gold medal swimmer Katie Ledecky, but I was fine with that.

Thus began my idea for *How Much Is Enough?* How does the concept of *enough* extend to dry land and other aspects of our lives? This book grew not only from my personal trials and tribulations, rabbit-hole research, and obsessive social media scrolling but also from conversations with many others who have attempted to redefine the concept of *enough* in their own lives.

Thought-provoking questions and "deeper dive" prompts are included in each chapter of this book. How does the concept of *enough* change as we age? Aside from material possessions, what does money buy? Was there a point in your childhood when you didn't feel you had enough? These and many more questions offer an opportunity for contemplation and conversation.

The moniker *interactive memoir* seems fitting. In this book I share some very personal stories about people, places, and things that have come and gone in my life. I am telling you these truths in the hopes of inspiring you to do the same. Through the reading and discussions of this book, along with my "How Much Is Enough?" Facebook group at https://facebook.com/howmuchisenoughbook, I hope to create a safe space for self-exploration with a soft, cushy community support system we will create together. As you answer the questions found throughout this book and explore deeper meaning with the exercises found at the end of each chapter, you will complete your own "Enough" Inventory.

I and everyone else joining the Enough community want to learn from you. I am turning my self-reflection outward. There is power in shared experiences. We will help each other by sharing our stories, suggestions, and solutions for how much is enough.

Let's continue this conversation together at https://facebook.com/howmuchisenoughbook.

CHAPTER 1

How Much Is Enough:

S P A C E

Our living spaces feel so much a part of our lives that stepping away from home for more than a day or two can feel like a personality transplant. An Airbnb rental feels like I'm moving into someone else's life, from eating breakfast cereal out of their colorful Fiesta ware bowls to wrapping my wet, naked body in their thick, thirsty towels as I climb out of their clawfoot tub. Even as I imagine an entirely new me, I simultaneously think about what parts of my own home I'm missing (my cozy, weighted-blanketed bed), and not missing (the uninvited and unwelcome resident mouse).

How does your mindset change when you change spaces?

I am writing this chapter about space while ensconced in a beautiful, three-story Victorian home my family has rented for a relaxing weekend getaway. An easy ninety-minute drive from Brooklyn takes us to Bellport, a charming beach community on Long Island. The desk where I'm writing faces a window overlooking the expansive front yard, where centuries-old oak trees drop their spindly branches onto bushy pines. This change of space, along with a change of scenery, feels rejuvenating.

It's a chilly, wooly cardigan kind of day. The sky is gray and the town is quiet. No one is lounging at the beach except for a cackling, gossiping gaggle of gulls. My cozy room sits above the wide wrap-around porch that offers two swings upholstered in sunny yellow fabrics. Wicker tables and chairs are haphazardly scattered on the porch as well, rearranged by the gusty winter winds.

Each spacious room of this home is luxuriously appointed with bold, colorful wallpaper, furnishings, and butter-soft blankets. In the kitchen, hand-hewn ceramic plates in bright shades of blue are displayed in intentionally gradient stacks on open, rough-hewn wood shelving.

The bookshelves give me a glimpse into the style and substance of the owners of this palatial residence, with the latest bestsellers, elegant, coffee table art books the size of actual coffee tables, and travel guides for dozens of exotic locales I will only visit in my wanderlust imagination.

Each floor of this home is full of unexpected, extravagant design elements. I imagine interior designers being led through the house by the homeowners, who are dramatically sweeping their marabou-cuffed caftan sleeves like magic wands, proclaiming, "More! More color! More accessories! More patterns! More everything!"

The children's room features floor-to-ceiling, hot-pink shelves filled with every imaginable toy: musical instruments; multicultural baby dolls swathed in diapers and onesies; and stacks of early childhood-friendly games, including Candyland and Chutes and Ladders. Mountains of precariously piled picture books, including my favorite Dr. Suess early readers, are stacked within reach of tiny hands. Grinning plush monkeys with Velcro hands grasp the floor-to-ceiling curtains. A dress-up cabinet includes every Disney princess gown. A pink metal bunk bed features a full-size bottom bunk overcrowded with giant stuffies, with barely enough room for my thirty-pound granddaughter to burrow in for the night.

If money were no object, how many homes would be enough for you?

A little Google snooping reveals that the owners of this house own twelve others, in Puerto Rico, Argentina, and throughout North America, which made me wonder how often they are actually here to rev up that dusty BMW parked in front of the detached double garage. I also wonder if their young daughters ever longed for any of the toys that live on those pink shelves.

* * *

As a child, I spent hours playing with my dollhouse. Okay, it wasn't actually a dollhouse. It was a bunch of cardboard boxes fashioned into a series of rooms with furniture made from milk cartons, contact paper, and fabric remnants. My family had no money for a fancy prefab dollhouse, but this wonky set-up was more than enough for me; I would not have traded it for all the hot-pink, plastic Barbie Dream Houses in the world. My dollhouse was an ideal escape hatch from my chaotic childhood and my initiation into the world of interior design. I loved the MacGyver meets Frank Gehry aesthetic that made these discards into a stylish dollhouse—further proof that children are much happier playing with the box than its contents.

I used to host a show for HGTV called *Fantasy Open House* that featured multi-million-dollar homes for sale, homes so large and exclusive that no For Sale signs would ever sully their front lawns. Any one of these houses would be more than enough for most of us to settle in for a lifetime of luxury. But these homes were often second, third, or fifth houses of the uber-wealthy. One such home in Aspen was being sold complete with all art, furnishings, and knickknacks included in the ten million dollar asking price. The real estate agent proclaimed, "You aren't just buying a house, you are buying a lifestyle"—as if the house itself wasn't enough.

Another memorable home we shot for the show was an exact replica of the White House built in an affluent suburb of Dallas. The owner proudly showed me around, pointing out all the striking, familiar details, from the oval office to the grand balconies. The bookshelves were stacked with books about past presidents and White House archi-tectural history. When I asked her if she felt at home when visiting the actual White House in Washington, DC, she admitted that she had never been. For her, fantasy outshined reality. Living in her very own White House replica was enough.

One *Fantasy Open House* home I will never forget was a true labor of love on the part of the man who had reluctantly put it on the market. He had spent over two decades traveling the world, snapping photos of the perfect archways, fireplace hearths, doorknobs, light fixtures, windows, tiles, and flooring. He'd bought garden statues and furnishings from every corner of the globe to include in this home. He even imported an entire tea house from Japan and had it rebuilt in a corner of his property. Throughout our day together, I was captivated by every story he lovingly told me about the personal travel memories associated with each design detail, along with all the memorable family events that had taken place there on the grounds.

His home was my fantasy. Oh, to have enough money, time, imagination, and resources to build my own dream house! At the end of the day, as my crew were packing up and the Arizona sun was setting on the glorious compound, I asked the bereft homeowner the obvious question: "Why are you selling this incredible home that you've put so much of your heart into?"

He answered glumly, "My wife doesn't like it."

It took extraordinary restraint on my part not to blurt out, "Leave the wife. Keep the house!"

●•●

How Do You Define Your Sense of Self Through Your Space?

Take a moment to reflect on all the places you have lived in your life. List them all, noting the following for each:

1. Your age and stage of life. Were you still living with your parents, out on your own, raising your own family, or empty-nesting?

2. Your financial status. Were you renting a room or living with a roommate because of finances? Had you saved enough to become a first-time homeowner? Built your dream home?
3. What you loved about the place. Dig deep to discover how it helped form your personality, your inner resilience, and perhaps your personal aesthetic.

Since graduating college, I have bought and renovated four homes. These homes varied in size, value, and circumstance. I always took pride in finding the worst house on the best street and relished the renovation process, thanks in no small part to excellent contractors and crew who felt like family—my dream family, not my real family, who have no idea how to build or fix anything.

As my two children grew up and my marriage ended, my definition of 'enough' space changed considerably. When my son's band practice moved from our garage to actual recording studios, I missed the twang of guitars tuning and the clatter of teenage boys raiding our kitchen cabinets for snacks. As my daughter packed up and headed off to college across the country, her visits home felt precious and fleeting.

When my bed became my own after thirty years of married life, my delayed adolescence informed many of my next housing decisions. Having married right out of college, this apartment would be my very first solo residence, a fifty-year old's single girl abode, inspired by all the happy single women from my favorite TV sitcoms who came before me, from Marlo Thomas and Mary Tyler

How have your life circumstances changed your living space requirements?

Moore to Murphy Brown. Oh, to have my very own Eldon! My fresh start was furnished with discards from friends and family, including wildly impractical white leather couches I never would have considered when I was a mom of young, sticky, magic marker-wielding kids. I loved every square inch of this beautiful, new beachfront condo, half the size of our family residence, but more than enough space to reinvent my life.

The sentimental heirlooms of our broken home went into a rented storage space that represented a temporary solution to the inevitable, which was ultimately discarding, donating, or disbursing stuff for which there is no space. Skis and boots from happy family vacations, never to be repeated. Toys and trikes for another generation of children, yet to be conceived, who may or not want to play with them. And stacks of photo albums capturing happy moments now eclipsed by our present, painful reality. When families downsize or split up like ours, renting storage space offers nothing more than a pricey hiding space.

* * *

I am a huge fan of the "Buy Nothing" groups on Facebook where neighborhood residents come together to share and disburse items no longer relevant or necessary in our current circumstance. Anything from wedding dresses that no longer hold happy memories, houseplants who have outgrown their windowsill, and toys our kids no longer covet are handed off to neighbors for free. Talk about a win-win.

In my Brooklyn neighborhood, it is understood that anything placed out on our stoop steps is free to anyone who can use it. We call it '*Shopping at Stoopman's.*' My granddaughter yelps with delight every time she sees an open box on the front steps. Once we came across a neighbor placing a giant plastic tub overflowing with Beanie Babies on her stoop. As my granddaughter rooted through to find her favorite, I looked up my neighbor and asked, "Not the investment you thought they would be?" She busted out laughing and my granddaughter thanked her for her new plush pet.

Since moving to Brooklyn, I've given up my car and a significant amount of square footage and reinvented my life in a new space. It is a compact garden apartment in a 128-year-old brownstone, and it provides enough indoor and outdoor space to feel like home.

I've never lived in New York before, nor lived in a building this old, complete with gracious ghosts who blast Taylor Swift on my Sonos speakers and turn on my electric teapot. This space is like nothing I ever imagined I'd be living in. The rooms are small and cozy, and my kitchen is a fraction of the size of my old one. Many of my go-to culinary tools live a vertical life now. Knives are stuck to a magnetic bar on my backsplash, and my pots and pans swing from wrought-iron hooks. The appliances are small but efficient enough that I can still prepare a multicourse dinner party or whip up meals for my family. My days of buying in bulk are over. I miss you, Costco, with your ottoman-sized packages of toilet paper and your Smart-Car sized jars of super-chunky peanut butter, but I can no longer accommodate your generous offerings. Daily treks to my neighborhood food co-op give me both exercise and sufficient groceries for meal prep without waste.

> If you've only lived in small spaces, do you think living in a larger space would feel decadent or discombobulating?

My daughter and her family live upstairs, and this upstairs–downstairs life suits us all just fine. And the commute home from a late-night babysitting gig is a pleasure: an easy jog down two flights of stairs, and I'm tucked into my cozy bed. I'm grateful for this space, the smallest since my dorm room yet extravagantly filled with love.

As I've observed from both my professional and personal life, having enough space is relative. Every time I returned from a trip shooting extravagant mansions for HGTV, I was always happy to unlock the door to my own home, my personal space, filled with enough family chaos, lingering unspecified kitchen aromas, and assorted handmade tchotchkes to feel welcoming and familiar. All this reminds me of the difference between a house and a home. It's more than just space; it's my life.

TAKE A DEEPER DIVE

What things make a new space feel like home?

List the personal possessions you treasure and explain what sensory memories travel with them and how they comfort you. Focus on small objects. These can be enough to invoke memories and fulfill wishes. Might a windowsill filled with lush potted plants remind you of a childhood backyard adventure?

Example: I like to travel with a Diptyque Baies candle. My daughter burned one in her college dorm room and again in her post-grad apartments. When I light mine, the familiar scent transports me to a deeply touching chapter of my life as a parent, when my teenage daughter emerged into the world as an ambitious young woman, creating her new independent life.

Do you have a storage space?

Of the items you have put in storage, list five that you access regularly and five you never want to see again. Add two columns to the right of each stored item. Head these columns *Storing* and *Hiding*. In the appropriate column, journal about the memories attached to each item.

Describe your dream space.

Here are several ways you might do this:

1. **Draw your dream space,** incorporating every detail—nothing is insignificant!
2. **Create a vision board on Pinterest** showcasing features you would love to have in your dream space, both interior and exterior.
3. **Create an actual blueprint drawing of your dream space,** either by hand or using Google Floor Plan, SketchUp, Smart Draw, or CAD software.
4. **Make this a creative writing project.** Write a story about your dream space, including fictional characters who are lucky enough to live in it. Would it be located in the mountains, the desert, or on the ocean? Would it be large enough to host extended friends and family, or would it be a cozy, intimate space just for you? Incorporate positive aspects of the space you grew up in, including natural elements that make you happy, and set it in a locale that inspires serenity. Feel free to furnish the space with evocative furnishings, food, and loved ones.

My dream space would definitely include many indoor–outdoor aspects, such as an outdoor shower, a massive eat-in kitchen, and an outdoor kitchen complete with a pizza oven. I also dream of a track-mounted bed that could be rolled onto a balcony overlooking the ocean so I could sleep indoors or out.

CHAPTER 2

How Much Is Enough:

A P P A R E L

A re your clothes a self-marketing billboard promoting a trend-setting life well lived? Or are you more like me, a spokesmodel for anything made chiefly of spandex and elastic waists? Perhaps you too are a sucker for fast fashion—trendy clothes that nourish our need for retail therapy without breaking the bank. If so, you know the feeling when Shein, Zara, or H&M beckons you hither, the next shiny must-have accessory swinging from its perfectly manicured finger as voices in your head whisper, "Don't think about sweatshops."

"Sucker," I mutter to myself as I click the item into my cart, although I usually come to my senses and remember that I have more than enough disposable fashion, *thankyouverymuch*.

As I watched an episode of the *Sex and the City* remake, "And Just Like That," I gasped with awe and wonderment as Carrie Bradshaw, Sarah Jessica Parker's character, revisits her wardrobe from the past two decades. Racks and racks of outrageous, extravagant, colorful ensembles line her living room, and Carrie lays hands on them the way an archaeologist delicately digs through the surface of Pompeii. What wonders do these dresses hold? What memories do they evoke? How many mature adult women now consider tutus acceptable streetwear? For me, the most amazing aspect of this tiptoe through her wardrobe is that everything appeared to be the exact same size. Not one woman I know has a closet that holds clothes of only one size, especially when the clothes span decades. And especially if that woman is fifty-plus, when most of our bodies bear little resemblance to our twenty-something selves.

Since my twenties, I have moved eight times. As a result, I did not have the luxury of being sentimental about my clothes. Each move inspired a ruthless edit of my wardrobe. I went through a brief vintage dress obsession in my twenties, wearing thrift-shop finds with tiny pearl buttons instead of zippers that I thought made me look timeless and unique. For a while, I saved these flouncy frocks, imagining they would actually be worth something someday, but alas, they did not stand the test of time, becoming tasty morsels for moths and other garment-loving vermin in my storage space.

When packing for my move to New York, I gave up all my "when I'm thinner" clothes and created a new, more practical capsule wardrobe for my new capsule-sized closet. I did pack a few legacy items, including my neon floral Betsy Johnson sweater, the very first high-end garment I bought with my own money. I hoped that my daughter would want to wear it, and she did.

> **What was the first article of clothing that gave you enough confidence to embrace your individuality?**

* * *

When I was a young girl dressed mainly in jeans and T-shirts, I couldn't wait to be older and wear fashionable clothes. There was no social media then, no tech-savvy fashionistas creating videos on YouTube, TikTok, and Instagram, extolling the importance of 'Five Outfit Fridays,' the need for 'Swiftie-wear' or 'Fire clothing.' My fashion influencers were Simplicity and Butterick sewing patterns. I collected their cardboard fashion posters of 1960s supermodels the way sports fans collected baseball cards. I coveted cut-outs of Jean Shrimpton, Cheryl Tiegs, and Twiggy modeling the latest sleeveless mini dresses or palazzo pantsuits. I would roam the aisles of my local fabric store, caressing bolts of velvety fabrics like they were my tall, dark, handsome dream dates.

I'd occasionally splurge on the actual sewing patterns, carefully unfolding the pale, crinkly pieces of printed tissue paper on our family's dark wood dining room table, the largest flat surface I could find. Then I carefully folded them back exactly as they came and put them back into the envelope. Because while I had a passionate *interest* in making my own clothes, I had absolutely no talent for actually sewing them. Fifty years have passed, and threading a bobbin remains a confounding mystery.

To be clear, I did not grow up in a household that had any consciousness for trendy fashion. There were too many kids and not enough money. My mother was not my fashion role model, as she often went years without buying clothes of her own so she could keep her four, ever-expanding children in clothes and shoes that fit. She was perpetually shopping for sturdy clothes for us, clothes that could potentially become a hand-me-down. Think Sears Toughskin jeans rather than Levi's button-fly bell-bottoms. Not only did I hate the look of Toughskins, but they were so thick and rigid I could barely sit down in them.

When did you first define your identity through apparel?

The second I was old enough, I got a job at Woodfield, my neighborhood mall, with the express purpose of making money to buy fashionable clothes. I made a point of befriending sales associates in stores with clothes I loved, with hopes they would offer me their employee discount when I was ready to blow my paycheck on something new. I counted the minutes until I could take my breaks, when I would pick a store and try on all the clothes I could find in my size, doing my own personalized trend-spotting. I was five feet, six inches in the sixth grade, so I prematurely moved from kid's sizes to women's, long before I had the body or the budget to actually own anything I was trying on.

I do have one vivid memory of a high fashion purchase that I truly wish I still owned. They were stacked platform sandals in baby-pink suede from the mall's fanciest department store, Marshall Field. The pale, butter-soft suede was utterly impractical for Chicago's schizophrenic seasons. Eschewing common sense, I saved my paychecks for months and bought them anyway. They were definitely my gateway drug into the world of fashion.

Pink suede platforms aside, I am not a shoe coveter or collector. I don't share my friend's joy of the hunt for a perfect pump, a fantastic flat, or a kitten heel. (I'm not even sure what a kitten heel is.) I have never had dedicated shoe shelves, never swathed them like newborns in tissue paper and labeled shoe boxes. I appreciate a beautiful pair of shoes, but I've never bought shoes as an investment, a status symbol, or a fashion statement.

Throughout my life, I've been the tallest girl with the biggest feet. As a ten-year-old with size ten feet, my mom convinced me that Dr. Scholl's sneakers were the bomb. Since then, comfort set the bar, and has, more often than not, upstaged style in my footwear.

That said, I do see the beauty in the design and engineering of shoes. I admire the challenge of balancing style with the function of all fifty-two intricate bones in my feet. I'm a big fan of sandals because I secretly believe my toes are one of my loveliest, most underappreciated physical features. I enjoy staring down at mine on summer subway rides and often wonder if anyone else does too.

At what age did comfort matter more than style?

I am fascinated by the evolution of the shoe. Based on cave art discovered in Altamira Cave in Spain from perhaps 13,000–15,000 years ago, we can trace how long humans have been wearing shoes. These cave drawings depict hunters wearing boots made of animal hides and fur. Who knew Uggs had such a primitive history?

As a lover of beautiful clothes and shoes, I often visited the expansive international fashion exhibition, *Christian Dior: Designer of Dreams*, when it was on display at the Brooklyn Art Museum. On one of my visits to the exhibit, I zeroed in on the shoes. They were outlandish, eclectic, and otherworldly. I felt like I was visiting a shoe zoo, a menagerie of rare, exotic species. Heels were constructed from geometric shapes, impractical curves, and clear acrylic spikes. The vivid colors were unlike anything I had seen in footwear, often paired with Dior's extravagant couture dresses. I kept asking myself, "Who would wear these shoes?" And, "What events take place in someone's life that would necessitate shoes as ornate and impractical as these?"

And don't even get me started about shoe prices. Exorbitant pricing of Dior shoes includes the Dior B23 high-top sneaker, which runs $1,200 a pair. Paying that much for a pair of gym shoes would never occur to me. I wince at paying retail for *anything*, especially shoes. I take pride in the knowledge that at any given time in my life, regardless of my income, at least 80 percent of the clothes and shoes in my closet were bought on sale. I'm that woman who cannot accept a compliment on what I'm wearing without sharing all the details. "Oh, this dress? I got it on sale 50 percent off at Nordstrom Rack. They have it in three colors. You should go! The sale runs through the weekend!"

Actor and fashion icon Katharine Hepburn said that, for her, getting into character always started with the shoes. Once she found her character's shoes, all the mannerisms fell into place, including her walk and her personality. I completely relate to this. The footwear I choose for my day says everything about how I will conduct myself. Lacing up gym shoes first thing in the morning urges me to get my workout done before I can talk myself out of it. Conversely, staying in slippers makes it easy to huddle up at home all day. "What? No! How can it be four p.m. already? I'm still in my slippers."

How often do you admire a pair of shoes or an article of clothing, look at the price tag, and think, Will I wear this enough to justify the price?

I am writing this afternoon in a pair of well-worn blue suede moccasins. I'll leave it up to you to figure out if I got to the gym today.

The high heels chapter of my life was brief and rather comical. Because I am so tall—usually as tall as or taller than my partner—high heels weren't required. Six years ago, I had a romantic partner who was crazy about heels and begged me to wear them. I was already several inches taller than him in bare feet, but he persisted. After my eyes stopped rolling to the back of my head, I acquiesced. I bought super-high, spiky heels and agreed to wear them only for him, and only when I was lying down. It was a creative compromise that happily met everyone's needs.

What percentage of your daily outfits are chosen to impress others?

I've heard people say that wearing heels makes your calves look great, but is that enough of a reason to wear these torture chambers? The two pairs of heels I currently own are zipped away in an under-the-bed storage bag. I'm no longer living a high-heeled life.

In my early years working as a stand-up comedian, I performed in Las Vegas in the comedy showroom at the Riviera Hotel. One floor above our showroom featured the spectacularly gorgeous entertainers at La Cage aux Folles. Female impersonators dressed to the nines strutted the stage in gorgeous gowns and impossibly high heels with more grace than I have ever seen a cisgender woman possess. Watching them was equal parts intimidating and awe inspiring. I understood the moment I saw the La Cage aux Folles show that powerful feminine energy is not just for women. We are all as beautiful as we feel.

Do you own pair of shoes or an article of clothing that can be enough to alter your mood or identity the minute you put them on?

What Is Your Earliest Memory of a Well-Dressed Person?

Describe this person in detail. Was it someone you knew personally or someone in the public eye? Jot down what impressed you most. Was it their clothes? The way they entered a room? The lingering impression they left behind? Does your memory of this person still inform your own clothing and accessory purchases, or has your sense of style changed as you've aged?

The opposite of sexy high heels shoes are Crocs, so ugly and yet so comfy. Ask any professional chef their favorite shoe to wear for their fourteen-hour shifts in the kitchen. Without hesitation, they will say Crocs.

Crocs may not go down in shoe history for being the ugliest comfy shoe. That distinction most likely goes to the "it" shoe of the 1970s, the Kalso Earth Shoe. Its creators, Raymond and Eleanor Jacobs, were inspired by a pair of sandals they bought during a trip to Copenhagen that cured their feet and back pain. Their version of that original sandal was made from wood, with a sunken heel intended to simulate the feeling of a bare foot sinking into soft ground. The shoe soon became a counterculture fashion statement, along with long hair and tie-dyed T-shirts. Oh, if I had only kept my

What is enough of a reason to buy a new item of clothing: Style? Comfort? Status? Revenge?

well-worn, much loved tan suede pair. The company dissolved in 1977, making the shoe an unlikely collectible. Who would have imagined that a pair would be found in the New York Metropolitan Museum of Art's permanent collection? Ask anyone in their fifties or sixties if they owned a pair of Earth Shoes. Chances are they'll give you a nostalgic grin and an enthusiastic nod.

Shoes have been the subject of adoration, fetishization, and repulsion. They have made millions for unlikely cobblers including Sara Jessica Parker, Jessica Simpson, and Khloé Kardashian, who stripped nude for the media campaign to launch her new line of shoes. This stunt seems to me like a nutty way to draw attention to footwear. I, like the rest of the world, have no recollection of the shoes she was wearing because I was looking for her artfully hidden nipples.

At this point in my life, I can say with confidence that I definitely have enough shoes. The pair I am most proud of is a well-worn pair of short brown leather boots that I bought fifteen years ago. I've had them resoled four times and marvel at how they've improved with age. We all should be so lucky.

* * *

My definition of an apparel discard, along with my perspective on the value of shoes, changed forever. In 2007, my brother-in-law Gilbert told us that many of the children in his homeland of Benin, West Africa, had no shoes, so my son, Sam, then fifteen, began a shoe drive with the hope of collecting a few bags of shoes for my sister and Gilbert to take back to Benin.

Sam's little shoe drive netted over fifteen hundred pairs of shoes. It was an amazing outpouring of generous donations that filled ten duffel bags and weighed a total of seven hundred pounds. To ensure these shoes would find new homes in this impoverished and politically corrupt terrain, we felt we had no choice but to personally accompany them to Benin. After bribing the customs agents at the airport with a bag of footwear, we were granted permission to enter the country to hand out shoes to children in need.

There were so many touching moments during the handouts. One eight-year-old child who had never owned a pair of shoes in his life gratefully accepted a pair of LA Gear light-up sneakers with utter disbelief. We handed a pair of soccer cleats to a teenager who had been playing soccer barefoot since he was five. We visited a classroom in a village where my sister used to teach, thinking we had enough shoes for every child in the class. However, one exceptionally tall boy's feet were too large for the kids' shoes we had brought. Without a second thought, Sam walked over to the boy standing in the corner, quietly measured his foot against the boy's, and proceeded to untie and remove his own Converse high-tops and help tie them onto this ecstatic student's feet. In that moment, I felt sure that my son's depth of compassion and understanding would be enough to guide him through the rest of his life.

I hope this inspires you to clean out your family closets and share discards with charitable organizations in your neighborhood. Don't forget to go through your coat closet. Many of us have coats we no longer wear that would mean a great deal to an unhoused resident in your community come winter. Several pairs of new socks would be a great addition to your apparel donations, as socks are the #1 clothing request at shelters.

* * *

In high school, I was oblivious to my physical attributes and felt very much like an outsider with my height and my bodacious curves. Most of my high school girlfriends were shorter, thinner, and flatter, and they found my 36C bra size impressive and aspirational. But there were never enough clothes in my size that seemed young and trendy enough for a high schooler built like Gina Lollobrigida.

As a high schooler newly transplanted to a Chicago suburb, I quickly observed that clothes were how my fellow students built their identities and their reputations. And while fashion fascinated me, I was clueless about my feminine appeal. My mom had always struggled with her weight and had horrible self-esteem, so I learned at a young age not to ask her for advice.

My feminine fashion mentor ended up being my theater teacher, Mr. Tom Smith. Mr. Smith was clearly a closeted gay man, although I was way too young and too out of touch with social constructs to connect the dots. He dressed in textbook 1970s schoolteacher attire, including baggy cardigans, oxford shirts, and wide-wale corduroy pants that you could hear before he entered the classroom.

Mr. Smith cast me as an ingenue in theater productions and selected my form-fitting costumes. He even taught me how to walk in heels. He helped me discover my femininity through the various roles he cast and clothed me for, and it was because of his vision that I found the self-confidence to embrace my power as a woman.

Fifteen years later, when I learned that Tom Smith had died of AIDS, I asked my former high school guidance counselor for his family's phone number. I spoke to his mother to offer my condolences, and we had a touching conversation. I was grateful I got the chance to pay him the respect he deserved. I told Mrs. Smith what her son meant to me and how he gave me more than enough reasons to fall in love with theater and define my personal style.

In college, working as a waitress at Ireland's, the local semi-fancy sit-down restaurant, I learned the financial power of dressing to impress. As much as it disgusted me, I knew that the tighter my uniform, the better the tips I would get. It was a tricky dilemma: stay true to my feminist principles, or make more money to finance my college years? I grinned and bared it until I got my rear end grabbed just as I was carrying a tray of four salads to a table. How they all fell directly on the lecherous customer's head is anyone's guess, but suffice it to say my days at Ireland's were numbered after that.

How old were you when you first looked in the mirror and believed you were attractive enough?

Years later, I was visiting my younger sister in Grenoble, France, where she was studying abroad. Who did I run into there but the star quarterback of my high school football team, a guy who had never given me so much as a sideways glance. He was in law school, working on his master's in international law. I was married and well into my twenties, and I felt emboldened to approach him and say hello. He recognized me immediately and greeted me enthusiastically. We talked late into the night and got caught up on what had happened in our lives since high school.

I decided to ask the question that had been rolling around in my mind for almost a decade. "Hey, Keith, why didn't any guys ask me out in high school?"

He paused, looked at me incredulously, and said, "Are you kidding? Guys I knew wanted to ask you out. You had enough swagger to pass as a sophisticated woman. You had so much confidence in the way you dressed. You were the star of every school play. We were all intimidated by you and always assumed you were dating older guys in Chicago."

I was uncharacteristically speechless. My high school self could never have imagined that answer.

When I began my career in comedy in Chicago, I dressed for a variety of performance spaces. When I was an ensemble actress with The Second City improv troupe, cast members were instructed to wear black so it would be easy to move in and out of a variety of spontaneous improvised characters. Clothes for stand-up gigs required more thought. Underground alternative clubs called for one vibe, glamorous showrooms another. And I knew that the minute I hit the stage, I would be judged by my appearance as well as my jokes. I had no interest in wearing a costume, or anything that would be distracting or suggestive. I admired Paula Poundstone's suit and tie, Judy Tenuta's

What's your definition of dressing for success?

25

kitschy prom-queen glam, and Judy Toll's signature big cherry earrings.

By the time I got to LA, stage clothes were a minor obsession. I experimented with a wide variety of looks, from simple black dresses to oversized Norma Kamali shoulder-padded suits, never really landing on one particular style. My mother had other ideas. To her, having a daughter in show business meant shopping for clothes she herself loved but would never wear. If it had beading, sequins, or any other bedazzled detail, she bought it for me. It was a very sweet gesture, but her picks were never appropriate for the LA comedy club scene.

Once I had kids, I quickly learned that mixing parenthood with a professional wardrobe yielded both precarious and hilarious results. When my babies were tiny, I left the house more than once after a good-bye hug with a Jackson Pollock–esque splatter of spit-up on my outfit that I didn't see (or smell) until I got to work.

Most clothing purchases in my first decade as a parent had one requirement: machine washable. As my kids grew older and wiped their hands and noses on me less often, I eased back into the world of high fashion, daring to wear dry-clean-only silks and linens. Slowly I emerged from my schleppy mom cocoon-wear into the au courant fashion universe, even re-subscribing to *Vogue* to see what the rest of the world had been wearing in my absence.

A brief flirtation with Fen-Phen, the miracle medication that helped me finally drop down to my pre-pregnancy weight, was exhilarating. I purged my closet of all my old clothes and was elated to move through the world in smaller sizes. Clothes had never fit so well, and I became a crazed clothes horse. There were more than enough options in an extravagant array of colors, textures, styles, and accessories. The simple act of tucking in my shirt was mind-boggling. And belts! So nice to see you again.

> **Do you feel the way your kids dress(ed) is a reflection of your parenting?**

Alas, this chapter was short-lived. Once Fen-Phen was found to cause heart problems, it was taken off the market, and my clothing slowly grew tighter. I was heartbroken. I felt like Charlie Gordon in *Flowers for Algernon,* who takes a medication that "cures" him of his mental disabilities only to find out that it's not effective enough to yield permanent results. Sadly, he, and I, had to return to our previous lives.

Throughout my kids' childhood, I let them pick out their own clothes. I had only two requirements: they needed to be clean and weather-appropriate. That was enough for me as their mom; anything beyond that was their call. Mismatched socks? No problem. Contrasting patterns? But of course. My kids had anti-Garanimals wardrobes: nothing matched. As a preteen, my son Sam went from psychedelic tie-dyed T-shirts to wearing all black virtually overnight. My daughter flirted with hip designer labels, mixing Kate Spade with colorful Custo Barcelona shirts. My kids learned early that clothes are a creative form of self-expression, and they made the most of their options.

Becoming single again in my fifties brought a slew of new wardrobe challenges. I was eager to flirt, date, and seek the company of men who knew nothing of my previous life as a wife and mom. I wanted to look sexy and alluring, but I also had to face reality. I found one or two go-to outfits that accomplished both. While I was open to dating younger men, I had no interest in deceptive dressing. Squeezing myself into tight, restrictive undergarments felt like pouring four gallons of pudding into a two-gallon tub. To be sure, clothes were essential for making a good impression, but ultimately the goal was to shed them, at which point my conquests would see the real me, sans shapewear.

What new chapter of life inspired you enough to change your personal style?

On the blustery winter day I am writing this, it is seventeen degrees in Brooklyn. When I must go out in this kind of weather, I bundle up in a knee-length puffer coat, gloves, a scarf, thick wool cap, and my obligatory pandemic KN95 mask. In this outfit there is very little chance that anyone I meet on the street will ask me out on a date. My winter gear basically serves as a dating firewall, preventing anyone from seeing the real me or catching my, "Hey, I'm available" vibe.

How do you define "dressing your age"?

Tonight, as I sit darning the underarm hole in my favorite sweater, I am reminded of my quality-over-quantity approach to clothes. This sweater, which I bought at a Barney's Warehouse sale over twenty years ago, is a men's hooded sweater made of a very warm, soft blend of gray-and-black-striped cashmere and wool, complete with a heavy-duty brass zipper. It is beautifully constructed and chic without being trendy. I pray I will have this sweater forever and that the moths that have nibbled on my other knitwear will never find this one delicious. I measure all potential sweater purchases against this sweater. If I could have just one sweater, this one would most certainly be enough.

TAKE A DEEPER DIVE

Look into your closet and say out loud, "I have enough clothes, enough shoes, enough accessories."

What emotions surface when you make this proclamation? Is this a true statement? Take a few moments to deeply survey the contents of your closet. Reflect on how much of it you actually wear. Twenty percent? Fifty percent? Now identify the clothing you love but haven't worn in a while and bring these to the front, most easily accessible point of entry. I call this _shopping in my closet._ It's always fun to rediscover something old and make it new again. And you didn't spend a dime!

Imagine you had to narrow your wardrobe down to six items of clothing. Which items would they be?

List these items, along with a detailed description of why they made the cut. Add an example of how this article of clothing has given meaning to your life. This will become your ideal packing list for upcoming travel!

Do you own garments or accessories that have equal parts sentimental value and functionality?

List each such item along with a story illustrating its sentimental value. Share an example of an occasion where you are most comfortable wearing the item.

Complete this sentence: If money were no object, I would wear . . .

What I find interesting about this exercise is that if we were in fact endlessly wealthy, would clothing matter more or less? If we had more than enough money, what would dressing for success even mean?

CHAPTER 3

How Much Is Enough:

E X E R C I S E

I f I lost a pound for every time I've asked myself whether I exercise enough, I would weigh nothing—actually, less than nothing. I have absolutely no idea how much is enough exercise for me, but I am 100 percent sure that whatever that amount is, I am not doing it. For me, exercise is laborious. I envy naturally active people: you know, the ones who opt for stairs over elevators, park their cars really far from the Target entrance, and love a long walk before bed. Coincidentally, these are also people who think of food as fuel. Physical exercise is their preferred mode of transportation. If this description resembles you, bravo! You won the genetic lottery and you will never be found on, in, or around my family tree.

When was the last time you exercised just for the fun of it, without wondering how many calories you burned or steps you took? The best natural exercisers are kids. Chasing after my five-year-old granddaughter reminds me of the pure joy of self-propulsion. She's like a pinball without the machine. I marvel at her flexibility. Five-year-olds don't work out. The minute they wake up in the morning, they are testing their physical limits. They fall down, go boom, do a quick assessment to see if they are really hurt or just need a hug, get back up, and throw themselves around the room again.

As kids get older, physical exercise is the way they measure independence. Here in New York, once you master the scooter, the sidewalks become your roadway to freedom, lengthening the imaginary tether between you and your parents. Then comes the bicycle. I can still remember the exhilaration I felt when I learned how to ride a two-wheeler. Once I felt confident enough sans training wheels, I traversed every block of my neighborhood and beyond on my bike. I was one of four rambunctious kids, and my mom was too overwhelmed to keep track of all our whereabouts. I knew that as long as I came home before dark and in time for dinner, my day was my own to go wherever my bike would take me. Of course bike riding was exercise, but to my nine-year-old self, it was simply a ticket to freedom—an escape from the chaos of my home and the stress of yet another confounding math worksheet.

No one in my family played organized sports. My parents never had much energy or interest in regular exercise, and neither of them ever signed us kids up for sports. For a brief time, my dad got inspired by President Kennedy's efforts toward youth fitness and would sporadically break out into bursts of calisthenics in the living room to try to motivate us. One of his favorite tactics was to blast the song "Chicken Fat," also known as "The Youth Fitness Song," commissioned by the President's Council on Youth Fitness. It was written by Broadway composer Meredith Willson and performed by Robert Preston, the star of one of Willson's best known musicals, *The Music Man*. We would gamely follow the song's prompts: "Push up, every morning TEN TIMES!" . . . "Give that chicken fat back to the chicken and don't be chicken again!" Eventually we all grew to hate the song and decided we loved lying on the couch and snacking more.

What do you consider your strongest physical ability?

What do you currently do for exercise? How has your exercise regime changed over the years?

In elementary school, in order to hang out with the cool kids, I tried skateboarding. There was no money to buy a skateboard, so I got the idea to take the wheels off an old pair of roller skates and attach them to a long piece of wood. I have no memory of who assembled this death contraption for me. I'm guessing it was my big brother, who had little experience with skateboarding, had no idea how dangerous it could be, and welcomed any opportunity to get me out of his room. One downhill run and two sprained wrists later, I switched to roller-skating at an indoor rink, where falling was much less precarious. Plus, the rink had a mirrored disco ball overhead and music booming over speakers. I loved the vibe of my neighborhood rink and had no idea I was exercising. It was enough just to be out with friends, circling the rink to Kool and the Gang at my own pace in my neon, rainbow knit leg warmers. Celebrate good times, come on!

Come summer, I embraced my life as a California kid and regularly took the bus to Zuma Beach to bodysurf. Armed only with a beach towel, a bologna sandwich, and a bottle of baby oil, I would return home water-logged, famished, and sunburned to a crisp. Sure, I got exercise, but I remember the primary attraction was being able to swoon at lifeguards all day and hang out in my happy place. I never once wondered if I was getting *enough* exercise.

* * *

Swimming, for me, has always been pure joy. When I was a young child, my mom considered the neighborhood public pool free summer camp. She'd pack me and my siblings sack lunches, drop us off early in the morning wearing bathing suits under warm jackets to beat the morning chill, and not pick us up until after three. Joining a water ballet team was the closest I ever got to participating in a competitive team sport. I loved the synchronized routines, and can still do a few of them today in my sixties. I proudly hold the family record for the most underwater somersaults in a row: eleven!

I'm pretty sure my love of swimming began as a very young child watching the undersea life at the aquarium. I would press my little face up to the glass and stand mesmerized at the rhythmic grace and weightless movement of each of the aquarium's inhabitants. Not much has changed today, except that now I am in a pool at the Y, still mesmerized by underwater life: my fellow swimmers of all ages and sizes swimming alongside me, lane after lane, their tattooed, varicose-veined thighs undulating, torsos turning with each stroke, hands fluttering and feet kicking through to the surface. I love how my mind takes its own laps as I swim, cycling through tasks, visualizing future adventures, revisiting past love affairs, along with grocery lists for meals I'll be cooking that week. I've never toweled off after a swim regretting having gone to the pool. For me, the simple sensation of moving my body through the water is enough to feel fit.

In my early twenties, I tried running. I loved the enthusiastic, supportive community I found at races and was in awe of the wide social and physical diversity of my fellow runners. I felt I was one of them, strong and invincible in my body. I was inspired by my dad, who completed his first marathon at the age of sixty-five. He too was drawn to the social aspect of running.

Running was a big part of my life until I got pregnant and my center of gravity changed dramatically. With every step, I felt like an elephant disco dancing. I stopped running and signed up for the Jane Fonda Maternity Workout. Jane's exercise videos were selling like crazy, so I figured her maternity classes would be a good way to stay flexible and meet other pregnant women. There I was, my baby belly protruding and my navel popping, lined up with other soon-to-be moms at the ballet barre in order of our due dates. I befriended Amy, the lovely woman next to me, and we gave birth two weeks apart. Now, both our babies have babies and Jane Fonda is in her eighties. Hey Jane, when are you coming out with a workout video for creaky knees?

The Big Three Rules I Know about Fitness

Cardio counts. Aim for thirty minutes a day most days of the week, but if thirty minutes feels like cruel and unusual punishment, try doing three ten-minute blasts instead. Get your heart pumping to get the most from your workout. How hard is hard enough to push yourself? A common rule of thumb for target heart rate is 220 minus your age.

Do some muscle-building exercises. You don't have to impress Arnold Schwarzenegger. How much weight is enough? Whatever amount you can lift eleven or twelve times and no more. If you can do fifteen or twenty reps, that's too easy and you won't build muscle. If you can manage only six or seven reps, that's too difficult and you might hurt yourself, which will be an ideal excuse to stop lifting, so don't go there, girlfriend. And you don't have to go to a gym. Lots of things around the house can serve as weights, including cans of crushed tomatoes (fourteen or twenty-eight ounces), bottles of fabric softener (forty-eight or fifty-six fluid ounces), or—my favorite—grandchildren (weight varies depending on age and time since last diaper change).

Get your doctor's okay before embarking on an exercise program. I am not a doctor, and I've never played one on TV.

Once I became a parent, I was determined to get my kids involved in organized sports to make sure they got enough exercise and time outdoors. We tried an AYSO (American Youth Soccer Organization) league, but our coaches ruined everything. Too many of them were trying to fulfill their own unrequited athletic dreams through the children. I was disturbed by the way they aggressively yelled at the kids. Coaches often got thrown out of the game by the referees, at whom they loudly, colorfully cursed within earshot of our children. In the car after every game, I eyed the kids nervously, waiting for one of them to ask, "Hey Mom, what's a dickhead?" We'd had enough, and we pulled our kids off the team.

I missed many of the families, again being more drawn to the social aspect of sport than the physical. I'd always rooted hardest for the kids who cared the least about winning the game. My favorite was a five-year-old named Cody whom we nicknamed, "Air Traffic Control Cody." Our soccer field was located near the Burbank Airport, and he spent most of his time on the field staring up at the sky and squealing with delight as planes swooped by. Just to watch the planes and be on the field with his buddies was enough sport for Cody.

* * *

For my fortieth birthday, my friend invited me to her home in Sun Valley, Idaho, and gave me a gift of a group ski lesson, my very first. It was a morning class. I got myself out of bed, dressed in my cloak of many layers, got strapped into my rental ski gear, and clumsily trudged over to the bunny hill. I arrived breathless, feeling I had completed my day's workout before the class even began. The class started with introductions and it was immediately obvious that the other "new" skiers, decades younger than me, had way more experience than I did. I was quickly left behind as the teacher led them down one run after another with no patience for my fearful ineptness and dramatic wipeouts that often had my skis flying off my boots in opposite directions.

After class, I felt completely dejected and had a good cry over my bowl of chili in the ski lodge. A different instructor approached me and started chatting me up. He asked why I was upset, and I repeated the sordid details of my humiliating morning. He told me there was no way he was going to let me leave the mountain this dejected and unhappy. He offered to take me up the mountain after lunch for a complimentary private lesson that would not end until I fell in love with skiing. He would not take no for an answer, and I was genuinely touched by his kindness. We headed back out for what turned out to be a transformative afternoon. He introduced me to the beauty of the ride up on the ski lift, encouraging me to inhale the crisp, clean mountain air and marvel at the uniqueness of each snowflake and the way the snow clung to the pine trees like cake frosting. We stood together at the top of the mountain and took in the magnificent view as the other skiers whooshed past us in a blur.

We took our time skiing down each run, stopping frequently for his gentle guidance, encouragement, and a lot of laughter. I became more confident and less self-conscious with each new trail we traversed, and by the end of the day, I was in love with skiing, and so grateful this kind man had enough time and patience for me.

* * *

Back on flat ground, emboldened by my success on the ski slope, I decided to train for my first marathon as a registered walker. I joined the Leukemia Team in Training organization as an extra incentive to stay on track. If I was going to ask people for donations, I certainly couldn't let them down by pooping out before the 26.2-mile finish line. In addition to the fitness benefits and the satisfaction of fundraising, I found that walking gave me quite a bit of time by myself for personal reflection and contemplation, a rare treat for a parent of two young kids. Training to walk takes twice as much time as training to run. A ten-mile training walk can take more than three and a half hours.

Many people laughed when I said I was a marathon walker, as if walking a marathon wasn't enough of an athletic feat. I quickly learned that walkers are the underdog athletes on the track. The truth is, I was more resilient and much stronger as a walker than I was as a runner. I was much more consistent with my training and suffered far fewer injuries. I've completed seven marathons and six half-marathons as a walker. During many races, usually around the halfway mark, I gingerly step over weekend runners writhing in pain from spasmodic cramping from overwhelming their bodies without adequate preparation.

For me, walking is enough. I often think about the tortoise and the hare and am content to plod along, one foot in front of the other, moving in the right direction. But make no mistake, I am competitive. My two guiding rules of the sport are (1) finish before dark and (2) make sure there is at least one person behind me at the end of the race.

This was never truer than during the San Francisco Nike Women's Marathon. I committed to walk this race to celebrate my fiftieth birthday, and as the race grew near, I made the difficult decision to end my thirty-year marriage. I invited my girlfriends to join me, and they showed up for me in every way. Over a dozen pals popped up along the route, and my dear friend Wendy walked the whole first half with me. Throughout the 26.2 miles, I was rarely alone. These beautiful women cheered me on, walked with me, pulled down their pants and peed beside me behind trees, kept me laughing, and supported me. Around mile twenty-two, when each step felt like I was hauling a ton of bricks, my dear friend Manette thoughtfully removed my fanny pack from my waist and carried it all the way to the finish line, lightening my load and putting some spring back into my step.

As I reached the finish line, I reminded myself that I did not need to be a runner to call myself an athlete, and I did not need to be married to feel loved and supported. I could indeed just put one foot in front of the other and that would be enough to move me in the right direction, towards my next, yet-to-be-written chapter of life.

It's Not Exercise, You Are Actually ...

1. Protecting the environment. Grab a trash bag and a pair of gloves and pick up trash on your next neighborhood walk.
2. Doing a cardio clean-up. Vacuum faster, speed wash your windows, mega mop your floor with vigorous upper body motion. You'll work up a sweat and your house will get cleaner, faster.
3. Saving money by walking or riding a bike to work instead of driving.
4. Falling deeper in love with your partner by having more sex.

The evidence for the health benefits of moderate physical activity is compelling. Studies conducted around the world report that completing just 150 minutes of moderate exercise per week can reduce our risk of dying by 25 percent compared to people who exercise less. By giving up a few hours of mindless social media scrolling, dating-app swiping, or TV watching, I found the time to walk and appreciate the pure upside potential of walking. Simply taking a walk is enough to lengthen my life. And stretchy athleisure wear is more than half of my wardrobe, so I'm already dressed for success.

As I review all that I've written here about exercise, I am impressed at my journey as an ever-evolving athlete. I never looked like an athlete or competed in a team sport, so I never really gave myself credit for all the different sports I tried and personal bests I achieved. And the variety of athletic endeavors I've written about here don't even include my adventures with spin classes, Zumba, Krav Maga, and tennis. How sad that I thought these activities weren't enough to classify me as "fit," and yet here I am now, a strong, healthy sixty-six-year-old with no debilitating physical ailments.

I am completely at peace with the fact that I'll never be on the cover of *Sports Illustrated* as a swimsuit model or an Olympic athlete. Now, if I can just figure out how to gracefully get up from the floor after doing a puzzle with my granddaughter. Perhaps it's time to head back to restorative yoga class, or, as I like to call it, active napping.

Do you consider walking enough of a workout?

TAKE A DEEPER DIVE

What nonprofessional person do you admire for their physical acumen?

Describe this person in detail. How old are they? What is your relationship to them? What about their physical prowess do you admire? Is theirs a natural ability or hard-earned? In addition to your admiration, do you also aspire to be like them?

Imagine you could win an Olympic medal in any sport, real or imagined. What would the sport be, and why has it captured your imagination?

If you are at all like me, you watch the Olympics in complete awe, captivated by the physical feats on display and well aware that if you tried to duplicate any of them, you'd completely embarrass yourself and most likely suffer grave injury. But what if there was a unique sport tailored just for you, ideal for your physical acumen? Describe this sport in detail, along with your likely competitors.

What physical accomplishment are you most proud of?

Instead of harshly judging yourself for what you can't accomplish physically, write about a physical achievement you are proud of. Do not compare this accomplishment with anyone else's. This is all yours, a personal, physical accomplishment that is enough to brag about with pride.

CHAPTER 4

How Much Is Enough:

CHILDHOOD

I've yet to meet someone who can honestly proclaim that they had an ideal childhood. Something, or perhaps someone, was missing from our lives, and these voids contribute to yearnings that often follow us into adulthood. Yet, when the topic of childhood comes up, most of us pretend there were no negatives. But does it have to be this way? Do we have to wear these fake smiles like bad toupees, always wondering if we are actually fooling everyone into thinking we've got a head full of lustrous locks, deep down knowing that no one is really buying it? Can we all remove our *toupee of shame* and finally feel free to be natural and honest about the downsides of our upbringings? I often reflect on my childhood history and ponder how it contributed, for better and worse, to my adult decisions. The question I often ponder: *Did my parents give me enough love and attention?* Did yours?

I have two grown, fully launched children. After their dad and I divorced during their teens, the kids and I worked hard to reinvent ourselves as a family of three. Being a parent is not always easy, but it has been, and remains, the best part of my life. Great jobs come and go; idyllic tropical vacations are over way too soon. The final bite of something yummy can make me cry. Wild romantic trysts are fleeting. But my kids are forever.

* * *

Fresh out of college, I had no interest in having children. My post-college life in Chicago was more than enough for me, and I embraced the exciting unknown. I got married at twenty to a man I felt confident would be a good dad someday. But we were busy launching our respective careers in comedy and advertising, and for ten years, we remained happily child-free, delighted *DINKS* (double income, no kids), much to my in-laws' chagrin. We enjoyed our weekly sushi splurges, designer handbags, and impulsive, all-inclusive resort getaways, and we knew full well there would be no such thing as disposable income once we had kids. Back then, I did not see the long game, how motherhood would transform my life over time. I was too immature to grasp the concept of a forever partner or to fathom how children could fit into our plans.

Was there pressure? Yes. Sending out a baby announcement with our new puppy Bob's photo inside did not amuse the extended family. But that sweet little golden retriever pup, our fur baby, unleashed more than enough responsibility for us. I admit it was a silly stall tactic, but it made us smile as we addressed and licked the envelopes.

I changed my mind about children when we left Chicago, along with our friends and family, and moved to California in 1984. I hit thirty, and we decided to start our family. I had read enough about the risks of waiting too long to get pregnant, and we knew we wanted two children so each one would have someone else who would intimately understand what it's like to have crazy parents like us.

> **At what age did you decide whether to start a family? Are you at peace today with your decision?**

To all adults reading this, in or out of partnerships, who made the conscious choice not to have children, I salute you. Bucking societal pressure and the incessant nosy nudging of family members can challenge even the most self-aware adults who have other ideas about what constitutes a happy family life. Hats off to you, and to all the beautiful "me time" you've enjoyed throughout your lives. The money you saved on dry cleaning and upholstery stain removal services will easily pay for that exotic two-door sportscar with bucket seats filled with well-rested adults instead of Pepperidge Farm goldfish crackers, crushed Cheerios, and half-melted gummies.

* * *

I have come to the conclusion that not everyone should be a parent, and I count my dad as one of them. From my vulnerable perspective as a child, I watched him struggle to make sense of his role as a parent. Today I observe parents pushing strollers through Manhattan streets, and it is painfully obvious to me which ones backed into parenting half-heartedly. I see them attempting to reason, cajole, discipline, and ultimately bribe their kids into doing what they want with disastrous results. I see the dark shade of exhaustion in their eyes and hear the brittle resentment in their voices. I watch their kids scream louder, cling harder, and succumb with the bereft resignation of soldiers lost in battle. I flash back to my own childhood and am reminded that, despite my parents' best efforts, I too did not get enough attention or affection to feel heard or seen.

My parents had four children because my mother was one of four. But was that enough of a reason? After her first baby was born, she went into postpartum depression that spiraled into a lifelong battle with bipolar mental illness. Once I grew up and became her caregiver, I often wondered how her life and her health would have benefited from a smaller family.

In your opinion, did your parents have enough children? Too many? Too few?

* * *

I grew up in the sixties in a very traditional family, where my dad was our sole breadwinner and was often on the road, traveling the country for his job. My mom stayed home and struggled to manage all the domestic duties. I can remember from a very young age observing how overwhelmed my mom was with this arrangement and how she wisely set coping mechanisms in place. Mornings were tough for her, so breakfast for the kids most days was self-serve: a row of cereal boxes and a carton of milk. I had an ongoing love affair with Captain Crunch and the golden, sweet final slurp of milk at the bottom of my bowl.

We moved around a lot because of my dad's career, so my mom made sure the houses we moved into were within walking distance of our respective schools. Anxious to get out of our hectic home, I desperately wanted to get into kindergarten a year early. The principal told my mother only advanced four-year-olds could join the class, so I hatched a plan to convince him that I could read. I asked my mom to read me the same story every night, and I worked to memorize the words until I could read the book to her as she turned each page. Thus I was able to convince the principal that I could 'read' this book, as well as by completing a wooden block puzzle at warp speed. Today, sixty-two years later, I can still recall every detail of this life-changing interview. It wasn't enough just to be a kid. I wanted to be a student.

My mother had enough self-awareness to know there was no way she would be able to rouse, dress, feed, and walk us all to school every day. As a result, we mastered independent habits that would horrify today's parents. At just four years old, I walked myself to kindergarten, located about ten minutes from our

> Was there a point in your childhood when you didn't feel you had enough? How did you manage that feeling?

home, often stopping to chat with the transient residents of the trailer park I used as a cut-through. Plenty of essential hygiene habits were abandoned. I still have scars on my back and arms from the rampant staph infections I battled as a result of not being bathed regularly. I bit my nails until they bled since there was no one to trim them, and unfortunately nail-biting became a stress-relieving habit that stretched well into my teens.

If you could pick anyone in the world to be your parents (not counting your own), who would you pick and why?

With four kids under seven, my mom white-knuckled us through childhood, often locking herself in the bathroom to compose herself and find precious moments of privacy. I vividly remember wiggling the locked doorknob and calling out to my mother through the walls. When she would not answer, I would lie on the floor and push my tiny fingers through the slit of light under the door to try to hold her hand, wanting to comfort her as well as establish the physical connection that I so desperately craved.

As an adult, I can only imagine her desperation and her frustration at not being able to manage motherhood better. This knowledge only fueled her insecurities and her mental illness. I am grateful that before she died I was able to reassure her that she had indeed been a very good mother and that I knew she did the best she could with the hand she was dealt. I know my words had even more meaning since by that time I was a mother maintaining my own precarious balancing act with two kids.

What do you remember most vividly about your childhood that you have carried into your role as a parent?

I decided I only wanted to have two children for one simple reason: I didn't want to be outnumbered. With two parents and two kids, I felt we had a fighting chance at sanity. I was grateful to have an easy time getting pregnant. I know that's not the case for everyone. I am acutely aware that I don't know the whole story of single-child families. I'm careful when I meet a family with one child that I don't use the word *just* or *only* in front of *one*. Maybe they have one child by choice, or maybe they can't have another child for any number of medical reasons that are certainly none of my business. One child can most definitely be enough.

If you are a parent, would you say you had enough children, or would you have liked to have more?

Growing up, my three siblings and I often overwhelmed and provoked my parents into fits of anger and exasperation. My family home was loud, chaotic, and unpredictable because of my mom's mental illness and my father's impatience and explosive temper.

In high school, I often escaped to my best friend Nancy's house. Nancy was one of ten children, and her family was a miraculous wonder to me. Nancy's parents could not have been more different from mine, throwing parties, smoking cigarettes, and expecting more self-sufficiency than my parents did. I loved playing Yahtzee with Nancy's mom and had mad crushes on several of her brothers. One night at Nancy's, we calculated the total length of time her mom had been pregnant: seven and a half years! I was shocked

How do you feel parenthood or the decision not to have children defines your day-to-day decisions?

and mystified at how she was able to stand up, let alone win at Yahtzee. Clearly I had not done well in my biology class.

I spent the majority of my now grown kids' childhoods wondering if I was a good enough parent. Was I spending enough time with them? Did they have enough or too many extracurricular activities? Did they have enough discipline? Did I make them eat enough vegetables? Did we laugh enough?

What Does a Good Enough Parent Look Like?

1. Reflecting back on your childhood, list the most positive memories of your childhood as they relate to your parents. In your opinion, did they:
2. Give you enough attention?
3. Bolster you with enough positive feedback and support?
4. Provide enough basic needs, like food, clothing, a safe home?
5. Encourage your educational and personal pursuits?

My children are completely different from each other and this was evident the minute they were born. My daughter came out tiny, with the most delicate fingers, toes, and nose I had ever seen on a newborn. She was born early, but not considered a preemie, even though her entire foot was smaller than my ring finger. My son was the opposite. He burst into the world large, loud, and alert. The first time we locked eyes, I felt as if I was staring at a wise old man I had known my whole life. He has always been like this, always mistaken for older than his age. He was also born with an obvious case of FOMO (fear of missing out). This guy wanted to be a part of everything. He didn't sleep through the night until he was four, just to make sure he didn't miss one minute of excitement.

Successive interrupted nights' sleep with my daughter had me in a panic. Sleep deprivation was a fate worse than death for me as a first-time parent. Willing a two-month-old insomniac to sleep was tantamount to withdrawing money from my own bank account and calling it a paycheck. It was different caring for my son, knowing he would be my last. I hunkered down with him, watched way too many midnight infomercials, and may or may not have ordered solar-powered yard gnomes, chandelier-sized earrings, and nonsensical kitchen appliances in my sleep-deprived haze.

Looking back, I am grateful for so many aspects of parenting: the family meals, the vacations, the bedtime stories, and the loud band practices. I have fond memories of chauffeuring the neighborhood carpool, especially the time the kids and their friends forgot I was in the car and revealed all sorts of valuable intel as they conversed in the back seat. I take pride in the fact that ours was a house where all kids felt safe, happy, and well fed. My fridge door was open to all, and my shoulder was available for anyone's adolescent tears. And there was laughter. So much laughter.

To relieve my own sporadic boredom as a parent, I invented activities that would delight and entertain me as well as my kids. We had Ninety-Nine Cent Store playdates, where I gave my kids and their friends each five dollars and half an hour to run the aisles of the store à la *Supermarket Sweep*. I loved seeing what each child bought. My son's friends often loaded up on odd tools, puzzles, and safety goggles, while my daughter's friends stocked up on cheap make-up and art supplies. And of course, candy—so much candy.

> **Do you feel you had enough fun with your children? Looking back, what would you do differently?**

One of my points of pride as a parent was

not permitting cursing in the house. My kids rarely heard their dad or I cuss, although we did plenty beyond closed doors. I told my kids it showed a lack of imagination as well as a lack of vocabulary. Their friends also had to follow the no-cursing rule when they came over. My kids were mercilessly mocked by their friends about this until it was time to pack up and move to our new home. I needed help, so I told my kids to tell their friends that Saturday was Cuss Day and that everyone who came over had my permission to cuss like a drunken sailor as long as they packed boxes at the same time. When I greeted them at the door with, "Hello, motherfucker, get your ass in here," they knew the day would be filled with profane and productive hilarity. We had a ball, and boxes got packed.

Who my kids are to each other now as adults is one of my greatest joys in life. My daughter told me the main reason she wanted to have two children of her own was that she couldn't imagine her life without her brother, whom she considers a trusted confidante and best friend. My daughter has two daughters, and I pray those girls grow up to have close ties like their mom and uncle do. And I vow to be there for my daughter as she parents her young children so she too can find the joy, the beauty, and the laughter amidst the mountains of broken toys, dirty diapers, and permanently stained designer duds.

TAKE A DEEPER DIVE

What was the best piece of advice your parents gave you?

Write it down and credit which parent gave it to you. How old were you when you received this sage wisdom? Did it carry enough weight to be life-changing for you? How have you applied it throughout your life? In addition to answering these questions, write down any advice you have given your own children that resonated enough to change their behavior.

If you chose not to have children, what was the most valuable advice you received to help you come to that decision?

Our culture puts an enormous amount of pressure on twenty- and thirty-somethings to have a family. Do you believe life without children can provide more than enough sense of familiar connection? If yes, share some examples of people you know who have created a sense of family sans children.

What advice would you give your fifteen-year-old self, knowing what you know today?

Everything felt so intense to me as a teenager. When I was fifteen, my dad got transferred again, and I had to leave all my friends in California to move back to Illinois. I thought my life was over and didn't speak to my father that entire summer. I wish I could tell that grief-stricken teen that everything would come together in surprisingly fulfilling ways. What would you share?

CHAPTER 5

How Much Is Enough:

F A M I L Y

C an all that we received from our family, both good and bad, actually be enough?

Ah, family. We all come from one, and I am guessing that 99.99 percent of us have used the word *crazy* at one time or another to describe our own. For better and/or worse, they made us who we are today. My family of birth was composed of four children and two parents who stayed semi-happily married until the ends of their lives. We were solid middle class and moved often for my dad's career, sometimes smack in the middle of a school year. Throughout my childhood, I felt financial strain and emotional turmoil, and I often wondered if my upbringing was better or worse than anyone else's.

Each of us has a different definition of what constitutes family. I am happy that traditional families are no longer clearly defined, and in my opinion, family members 'of choice' can be far more intimate than blood. Chosen family members are truly magical people who come into our lives with all the love, emotional connection, and understanding that blood relations may or may not provide, without the historical familial entanglements or the wonky physical family resemblances (Hello hook nose!), that you don't really appreciate anyway. If you are part of a traditional family, chances are your relations hold hard and

> As a child, did you long for kin different than your own, or did you receive more than enough love and support from your family of origin?

fast to certain rituals and traditions and believe that these experiences are what keeps everyone close and intact. I'm not saying they are wrong, but I'd like to explore ways we can redefine family and answer this question: Is it possible to get enough love and approval from those who meet the strict legal definition of family?

* * *

My move from Los Angeles to Brooklyn in my sixty-fifth year was a bold experiment that has turned into a constant reminder of how important regular family contact can be. I am well aware that daily contact with adult children is rare and not always a preferred arrangement. Very few of my friends would live under the same roof as their grown children. They also admit their children would most likely not invite them into this cozy setup for any number of reasons.

My daughter and her husband moved from California to New York and bought a brownstone. It includes a separate garden-level apartment, which they offered to me in exchange for afternoon childcare for my adorable granddaughter. Desperate to be close to her and play an intimate role in her life, I left everything familiar behind in California: my home, job, friends, car, along with my wonderful adult son who graciously supported my decision by saying, "I want you; they need you. Go."

My daughter, my son-in-law, and I have settled into a lovely cohab existence. In addition to providing afternoon childcare and semi-regular weekend babysitting, I also prepare and host dinner several nights a week, which takes pressure off of them at the end of their busy work days. I love to cook and hated cooking for one, so this has been a win-win for everyone. As a bonus, research shows there are many health benefits to eating with others. A Harvard university public health study reports that our diets improve when we eat together; for example, we eat more fresh fruits and vegetables and consume less fast-food.

Not that I serve every dinner on fancy china plates, but I never feel that food tastes as good when it's eaten out of a disposable container or while standing alone hunched over the sink. A nonprofit organization called The Family Dinner Project has conducted over three decades of behavioral research that reveals families who have regular meals together experience enhanced physical health, social-emotional skills, and success in school. I really do love cooking for my family, and I get help doing the dishes and using up leftovers, which I always appreciate.

* * *

Many holiday traditions include a large family meal. When parents are divorced, as my children's are, planning these get-togethers can be as stressful as an air traffic controller working an overnight double shift the day after Lasik eye surgery. As I watch my kids dedicate the lion's share of their annual vacation days to family visits, I feel a mix of pride at their dedication and sadness that so little of their free time is their own for self-indulgence and separation from familial obligations. I've made a conscious effort not to guilt my kids around holidays. I want them to have an opportunity to build their own holiday traditions, with or without me. It should be their choice.

I doubt there is anyone reading this who hasn't had to suppress the urge to yell, "Enough!" or something more colorful as a relative yammered on at a holiday meal. I hear more and more about families who can no longer celebrate holidays together because of an extreme rift over politics or Covid vaccination status. And if, like me, you've had a family member with a substance abuse problem, you have intimate knowledge of how easily a simple get-together can turn into World War III. The idyllic Thanksgiving meal depicted in Norman Rockwell's iconic 1943 painting, *Freedom*

How often have you thought (or said) "Enough!" during a family conversation?

From Want, is rarer than your Facebook feed would have you believe.

What would a 2023 version of this painting look like? I'm guessing at least half the family members would be staring down at their phones and the remaining dinner guests would be drunkenly debating the world's problems with their outside voices. The matriarch would not be in a spotless, crisp, white apron. She'd most likely be rocking a colorful collage of pan drippings, sweet potatoes, and children's handprints smeared across her blouse like a gastronomic Rorschach test.

Money is also a common culprit for fracturing families. I've yet to meet a family without a sibling experiencing some level of jealousy, resentment, or entitlement over money.

* * *

How can we find a way to communicate with difficult relatives, and should we even try? I have spent countless hours in my life combing the greeting card aisle trying to find a card that expresses how I feel about a challenging family member who is celebrating a momentous event. Mother's and Father's Day cards can be especially problematic if you are on the outs with one or both. It's a strange feeling, flipping open one card after another, shaking your head and sighing, *nope . . . nope . . . nope,* until you find the blandest, most generic, unemotional card that fulfills the mission of marking an event without committing to a misguided sentiment. In the thirty years I was married, I never found a Mother's Day card that captured the complicated feelings I had for my mother-in-law. Thankfully, e-cards seem to be a much easier, more customizable approach these days—plus you save on postage.

How did your grandparents influence your parents' parenting of you?

Who is your family of choice? When family are unavailable or undesired, who are your go-to people? That tribe of people who love and accept you unconditionally can be the garden where you magnificently bloom. Too often, incessant friction with a parent leaves a callus on the heart, hardening and changing a person in damaging ways. I've met many people who say they fled their family's abuse, alcoholism, incessant judgment, or indifference and found salvation and a true home with their family of choice.

Where Does One Find a Family of Choice?

1. Spiritual communities. Many people find chosen family members through their place of worship, thanks to services and organized social activities. Members of twelve-step programs often find their chosen family in the meetings, long chats over coffee where members gather for personal conversation, and where deep connections are formed.
2. School. Classmates, roommates, and even teachers often become a family of choice when you are away from home. Often those relationships become much more intimate and life changing than relationships with relatives.
3. The neighborhood. How well do you know your neighbors? During the pandemic, many people started reaching out to neighbors, especially those who were living alone. Neighborhood rituals created a sense of connection despite living in quarantine. I found it touching how people cared for each other during that trauma and how often those connections deepened and endured long after the masks came off.

4. The gym. Attending the same yoga, spin, aqua aerobics, or Zumba class at the same time every week creates a sense of familiarity and community. And a shared passion and commitment to healthy self-care can be the ideal environment to find a close connection.

5. The workplace. This one might seem a bit precarious, since the stakes feel higher when a hierarchy exists, work must get done, and money gets earned. But the truth is many of us spend more waking hours with coworkers than some of our loved ones. Professional relationships can become personal under the right circumstances.

I recently read a touching essay by a woman who consciously estranged herself from her parents. She decided she was done with their drunken tirades, body-shaming, financial meddling, and incessant helicoptering, and she courageously walked away. She reports that her life has become immeasurably better since she made the break. I doubt there's an eye-rolling, petulant teen on this planet who hasn't had fantasies of cutting their parents loose, but this was a grown woman who'd simply had enough.

Have you had enough of a family member's behavior and consciously ended your relationship with them?

* * *

When I was a child, I believe my parents had only the best of intentions when they created the Sunday Family Meetings. This meeting usually took place at breakfast when we were all home and around the table. Every child, regardless of age, got a chance to speak uninterrupted, and when everyone was done, we could comment on what another family member had shared. In theory this is a great idea, but the execution was often a disaster. The older kids defensively ganged up on the younger ones, with my little brother getting the brunt of blame for things he may or may not have done. Imagine the current disparate United States Senate hearings served with lox, bagels, and strawberry-rhubarb Jello molds, and you've got our Sunday Family Meetings. Petty he-said-she-said bickering and filibustering invariably broke out and proceedings usually ended with my dad yelling at all of us and storming from the table.

My father was truly at a loss when it came to parenting young kids. He had no patience for our childish behavior, even though we were in fact children. He lost his temper loudly and often. One summer when I was nine, at my mother's insistence, he took each of us on one solo date. My mom could tell we were distancing ourselves from our dad and his unpredictable anger, and she thought this might be a way for us to reconnect. I remember my date with my dad vividly. Our conversation was easy and fun, and he remained very calm and very loving throughout. He even bought me an oversized troll doll and white leather go-go boots—an uncharacteristically extravagant gesture, given that he was usually stressed about money against frivolous purchases. I wonder if I remember this date so vividly because of that combination of

What are the most impactful lessons you learned from your family?

feeling attentively heard and showered with gifts, both extremely rare events during my childhood.

My siblings and I were quite belligerent in our behavior toward each other, and it's impossible to say why. You would think that with all the geographical moves our family made throughout our childhoods, we kids would have clung to each other for support and friendship. But that was not the case. Perhaps it was our age difference, or that we were left largely on our own too young, without empathic modeling from our parents.

We often got in real trouble—like the time I was four, and my six-year-old brother set fire to my bed while I was in it. I screamed bloody murder, unable to get out, and my parents had to call the fire department. After my smoldering mattress was removed from the house, one of the firefighters told my parents that unless they gave my brother a visceral experience of what fire can do, he would become a pyromaniac and do even more damage. While my mother cried, my dad and the firefighter ran a lighter under my brother's arm for a first-degree singe, enough to cure him from ever playing with fire again.

My siblings and I are all very different, and we have been since we were small. It's as if we were cast in roles: my older brother, always the biggest in his class and often bullied for his size; my sister, with her impressive brain, who instantly charmed all her teachers and went on to master multiple languages; and my little brother, acting out every which way in a futile attempt to garner the attention he needed. I just wanted out, both physically and emotionally. The theater department became my exit plan. I wholeheartedly embodied every role I was cast in, from a cackling, "Pick-a-Little, Talk-a-Little" lady in *The Music Man* to the time-traveling, death-defying Emily in *Our Town*. Theater fueled my overactive imagination, offered an eccentric community of

What role did you play in your family dynamic?

loveable, like-minded thespians, and provided a welcome respite from my real-life drama back home.

While I was pregnant with my first child, I read Shirley MacLaine's book, *Out on a Limb*. She wrote about her spiritual belief that children choose their parents. I had never thought about this. If that were true, why had I chosen my parents? This got my mind racing. If I could actually have chosen my parents, who would have topped the list: actors, politicians, rock stars? It exhausted me to contemplate these scenarios. It felt like trying on a pile of sparkly designer gowns that all itched and had broken zippers. Nothing fit right, and I realized that my real-life parents were enough, more than enough for me.

* * *

Throughout her life, my mother had a clear, unwavering sense of right and wrong. As a University of Illinois student in the late 1940s, she was an activist who organized civil rights demonstrations at a restaurant that wouldn't serve Black customers. When she graduated college with a degree in education, she headed back to her hometown of Chicago to work in a school in an underserved neighborhood on the South Side. In 1953, a year before she met my father, she took the first step toward her dream of teaching around the world: she applied to teach abroad in schools for US Army families. She was turned down, and she was sure it was because of her civil disobedience. After she died, my brother did some digging through the Freedom of Information Act and discovered that she did indeed have a big fat FBI file personally initiated by J. Edgar Hoover. We could not be prouder. I'm so grateful that my

Do you believe you chose your parents?

granddaughter is named after her. May my mother's strong, principled spirit live on in my daughter's beautiful girl.

* * *

As our parents aged, family roles shifted, and my siblings and I took more and more responsibility for their care. My mother died first, giving me the opportunity to grow closer to my father. After my mother died, dementia slowly robbed my dad of his memory, As we moved him from one level of memory care to another, we took care to keep his surroundings familiar, even making sure all his pictures were hung the exact same way on each new set of walls. Think *Architectural Digest* à la *Groundhog's Day*.

What aspect of your personality do you attribute to your family?

I planned many excursions with my dad to invoke memories of his previously bustling social life. He was my date for what turned out to be his last New Year's Eve celebration. I smiled at him across the table where he sat in his shiny gold cardboard top hat, marveling at how far we had come as a father/daughter combo. When I was a self-styled hip adolescent, I was contemptuous of his geeky, stuck-in-the-sixties bespectacled vibe, complete with short-sleeved dress shirts and his beloved plastic pocket protector. He had no patience or respect for popular culture, which I consumed hungrily from any source I could find. In short, we had nothing in common. And yet here we were, fifty years later, all dolled up in our contrasting party couture, seated at a prime table at the first seating of an abundant, all-you-can-eat seafood buffet in a swanky restaurant with live music festooned with New Year's Eve decor. He happily returned to the buffet several times, kibitzed with the musicians, and really had a ball.

After his third dessert, he sighed contentedly, looked across the table at me, and said, "I can't remember the last time I had this much fun and stayed out this late. I'm bushed. Let's head home." It was 7:15 p.m., and I had him back home by 7:30 p.m. The Times Square ball drop was only in his dreams. Happy New Year!

In my parents' final years of life, my kids often commented how touched they were by my attentiveness to their grandparents, to which I would invariably reply, "Take notes. In thirty years, that'll be me."

TAKE A DEEPER DIVE

Did you ever wish you ever had someone else's parents?

I'd wager that most of us at times wished for different parents. Do you remember how old you were and what circumstances exasperated you enough to want to trade your parents for a different set? Write about this awakening and the thought process that had you contemplate this change. Who had parents you coveted? What made them so attractive? List their attributes. Were they more fun, generous, permissive, or absent? How has your concept of the ideal parent changed with age? If you are now a parent, which of your ideal parents' attributes did you include in your parenting arsenal?

What family traits would you like to be passed down to the next generation?

As adults, we can craft our own personas because of and sometimes in spite of our biology and our upbringing. List the traits you got from your family that you feel most proud of—the qualities you hope the next generation will embody.

***Would you be friends with your sibling(s)
today if you weren't related by blood?***

When siblings reach adulthood, they are faced with the complicated decision of what sort of connection they want to maintain. Take a moment to think about each of your siblings. List qualities of theirs you admire. Also list qualities that pose a challenge. Are these qualities enough to forge a lifelong friendship as adults?

CHAPTER 6

How Much Is Enough:

H E A L T H

As I contemplate the topic of health, I am typing on my laptop in a fifteen-point font size, and I still need my glasses to see the text clearly. I remember in my early forties feeling so proud, and maybe a little cocky, about the fact that I had never needed glasses even though both my parents and one of my siblings wore them. I was an insatiable reader, and I never remembered my eyes going blurry or feeling fatigued. And then one day, BAM! It was as if I had woken up from a twenty-four hour bender with a fine mesh shower curtain wrapped around my head. I couldn't read anything without squinting. I put vanity aside and went to the eye doctor to get checked.

Vision is a basic, profound aspect of health. There is no such thing as *good enough* eyesight. When my son, Sam, was in second grade, he had already earned a reputation as a restless learner, often losing interest and acting out in class. One of his teachers suggested I get his eyes checked. I was surprised at this recommendation. Our family pediatrician had given him the basic exam during all his annual physicals with no concerning results. I decided to take Sam to a pediatric ophthalmologist, who shared a very different diagnosis. We learned Sam had horrible vision and needed corrective lenses, including prisms, to see clearly. When I held his new pair of prescription glasses up to my eyes, I almost started crying. What kind of negligent parent lets their kid walk around with this degree of vision impairment? I might as well have been sending him to school blindfolded.

The ability to hear is often overlooked as well. When Sam was six, we grew tired of watching him incessantly pound every surface in the house, and we bought him his first professional snare drum. And yes,

I was vigilant about keeping a supply of ear plugs close by. We had him fitted with custom headphones and convinced him to wear them with the promise that he would be rewarded with a long, successful music career if he kept his hearing sharp. Thankfully, he complied and is now enjoying that promised career.

* * *

Our collective health seems to be a primary topic of conversation these days. Since Covid reared its fuzzy, round, red polka-dotted head, every physical symptom is endlessly analyzed, self-diagnosed, and feared as potentially fatal. Looking back at the first year of the pandemic, I was a wreck. I questioned everywhere I went, everything I ate, and everyone I touched. After I contemplated hand washing all my groceries, I realized no one was considered neurotic in the early days of Covid.

I have never leaned toward hypochondria. I'm not only a 'glass half-full' kind of girl, I'm also a 'Hey, look, I've got water in my glass' kind of girl. But Covid knocked me for a loop. It wasn't just my health I was worried about, it was my loved ones, my friends, and the world. It was impossible to get my arms around the scope of this pandemic. I worked hard to keep the focus on myself and strike that tenuous balance of living my life with caution and consideration for those around me. I went from being social and out in the world to a virtual shut-in, completely out of my comfort zone, but what else could we do? As time went on, we all found our new normal. What's enough caution? What's the right balance of obsessive hand washing, house cleaning, and social distancing?

Reflecting back to the year 2020, would you say you took enough health precautions?

I have been quite fortunate to have not personally faced any significant ongoing health challenges, including my thankfully uneventful bout with Covid. I've been medically designated as overweight for the past two decades, but aside from high cholesterol and osteoarthritic knees, I haven't had any health challenges because of my extra pounds. Two of my three siblings have also struggled to lose weight, and I suppose we can blame genetics, since our parents were also overweight. Yes, we have a genetic propensity to weigh more, but I also love to cook and to eat, so there's that.

* * *

Chronic illness presents itself in a variety of unique maladies, thanks in no small part to family, behavior, and the environment. Growing up with a mentally ill parent gave me an uncomfortable front row seat for the erratic life a chronically ill person must manage. Starting each day not knowing what mood my mother would be in was like playing a demented game of *Let's Make a Deal*, one of many of my mom's favorite game shows. Except we never got to pick what was behind door number one or peek behind the curtain. And there was no beautiful model with sweeping gestures, encouraging us to make a good choice. My bipolar mom cycled unpredictably between mania and depression. As children, we were perpetually poised to pivot accordingly.

To understand the genetic propensity toward mental illness, take a gander at my mother's family tree. Three of the four children in her family suffered life-long bouts with mania, depression, or bipolar disorder. And many of their children have also been diagnosed with mental illness. Of course in the 1940s and '50s, there was very little understanding of mental illness, so treatment was spotty at best. My mother didn't see a psychiatrist until she was twenty-eight, after giving birth to her first child. She was hit hard with what we now know to be postpartum depression. Her very first visit to a psychiatrist was a disaster. He dozed off while she was talking to him. She got up and left, totally dejected, and received no treatment for her mental illness until she was hospitalized two decades later after a psychotic episode. My beautiful mother spent the rest of her life in and out of psychiatric facilities and on a precarious and often ineffective seesaw of psychotropic medications.

Know Your Family Medical Information— Past, Present, and Future

Here is a list to get you started thinking about your family's medical history:

1. Genetics. How many of your health challenges do you attribute to family genetics? I've had to take an inventory of what physical and mental traits have been passed down, either by nature or nurture. Either way, I look at my siblings and there are undeniable health challenges we all share. What are yours? If you aren't sure, or are adopted, are you able to find relevant medical history from your birth parents?

2. Vaccinations. Are you and your loved ones current on all vaccinations? I'm aware that this topic can divide families, but the science is compelling and history has proven that vaccinations have a huge positive impact on global health. Make sure you have current electronic records of all immunizations for every member of your family.

3. DNR. This will be one of the toughest conversations to have with family members, but it is important and deeply respectful to create a DNR (Do Not Resuscitate). This legal document clearly details how much CPR

(cardiopulmonary resuscitation) a person wants should their heart or breathing stop and they are unable to make these decisions for themselves in crucial life and death moments.

We have so much to learn about the brain, perhaps the most mysterious part of our anatomy. And there are so many degrees of wellness when it comes to mental health. There are miles between feeling good enough to function in the world and achieving peak performance.

* * *

Perhaps the most mysterious and scary diagnosis is cancer. Even when it is caught at its earliest stage, patients can't help but hear, "Get your affairs in order," whether anyone says it out loud or not. Cancer seems to strike so randomly, with no justice or mercy. Why do healthy nonsmokers get lung cancer? Why do people who diligently eat all the right foods and avoid the bad ones get stomach cancer? I remain in awe of my friends who have fought cancer and won, resplendent with the victorious battle scars where tumors and shunts were removed from their bodies. They took an aggressive, active role in their own treatment, questioning diagnoses, seeking second and third opinions, mixing Eastern and Western medicinal approaches, and surrounding

Why don't we do a quick check-in: How are you feeling today? Are you healthy enough to enjoy the day?

their sick bed with love and positive energy. To me, these friends are a shining light of resilience and rocky road-tested health.

* * *

"Did you sleep well?" is a common morning greeting from a caring loved one. Getting good sleep is a key factor in optimum mental and physical health. And my bed is my favorite hiding place, fitted with a mattress with just the right amount of spring and a duvet with just enough weight to envelop me in a pretend boyfriend hug. Putting myself to bed early or lingering once the sun rises is among my favorite luxuries in life. I average six to seven hours of sleep a night, interrupted often by vivid dreams (rarely romantic, usually mundane), or insistent nudges from my bladder. I sleep so lightly that I find silence deafening. I augment the silence with a trio of distracting sounds, including a desk fan, an air filter, and my own audible, raspy breathing. Getting eight hours of sleep feels almost intoxicating, like I just received a magic drug that has simultaneously relaxed, restored, and invigorated me. When my kids were little, sleep deprivation felt like a form of torture. It was hard enough to keep up with them on a decent night's sleep. A bad night's sleep could bring me to tears. Once they began sleeping through the night, I made my own sleep a priority, passing up countless invitations for nighttime fun. It just wasn't worth it. Getting good, consistent sleep was enough.

My mother managed her depression with sleep. She treated it like the flu. If she could just sleep until she felt better, she wouldn't have to manage all the negative feelings and physical debilitations that came with her depression. Sometimes she would sleep for days at a time as we'd adjust her medicine and wait for her to return to a state of normalcy. But that too would be fleeting because once she felt better, she'd convince herself she didn't need her medicine anymore, become manic, and then crash again into depression. I will never forget how painful it was to watch her cycle through all of this. Being her caretaker, I often felt like I was strapped into the seat next to her on a whiplash-inducing roller coaster. I can only imagine how it must have felt inside her head.

Caring for my father brought a whole new set of challenges. When my mother died suddenly from a stroke, my dad moved back to Leisure World in Seal Beach, California, where he had lived with my mom before her chronic health issues required additional care. My dad loved living at Leisure World and took advantage of many of the social opportunities offered to their residents. He began each day with 7:30 a.m. poker games, attended weekly concerts and dances, and hopped free bus rides to local casinos. All of this helped him fill the void left by my mother's passing.

What is your personal definition of "good enough" health?

When my father was eighty-five, we brought him Benny, a scruffy, extremely affectionate rescue dog, as a Father's Day gift. Benny became my dad's constant companion, or as he described him, "my chick magnet." He walked Benny several times a day. The exercise was great for both of them, and Benny turned out to be an eager wing-mutt, literally sniffing out my dad's potential romantic conquests. My dad met lots of lovely women with Benny in tow. But as dementia took hold of my father, he'd often get lost while walking Benny, and we soon realized he needed to move to a new community that could keep him safe as his memory progressively faded.

Has your parents' health—good or bad—been enough of an inspiration to impact your self-care?

* * *

We expect our parents' health to decline as they age, but nothing can prepare you for a sick child. My then fifteen-year-old son Sam and I traveled to Benin, West Africa, with my sister and brother-in-law to deliver shoes to children throughout the country. While the shoes were deeply appreciated by children who had never owned a pair, shoes were simply not enough to make a dent in the myriad of challenges the Beninese face on a daily basis. We were forever changed by the images, the people, and the relentless challenging public health issues that plague virtually every citizen of this impoverished country. No one escapes. Not even us.

Ten days after we returned home to LA, we were almost giddy over our good health. Careful eating, preventive medications, and diligent hand washing gave us the illusion that we were out of harm's way. Hey, we got our vaccinations in advance of our travels and dutifully followed instructions. What could go wrong?

And then Sam got sick, ferociously ill with mysterious symptoms. First his eyes itched; then they filled with blood. Then his joints started swelling. Then he stopped walking and stopped sleeping because of the chronic, unrelenting pain that coursed through his body. Doctor after doctor gave up on Sam after scratching their heads and consulting medical textbooks in front of us with panicked page-turning that didn't exactly fill either of us with confidence.

Sitting in the waiting room of one rheumatologist's office for over two hours, listening to the audible pain coming from the dozen or so other patients in crippling states of anguished exhaustion, was like being forced to watch the bloodiest scene from a horror movie. My son was one of these patients with chronic, mysterious pain, willing to wait it out, desperate for a diagnosis. It was decided by committee that Sam had developed a rare autoimmune disorder, a reactive form of arthritis called ankylosing spondylitis. Sam's body had turned on itself with a vengeance.

"Well, Sam," the rheumatologist explained, "it's going to be about six months before you'll be up and around again, and there is every chance you will develop this again if you ever let an infection fester in your body for any length of time." The off-handed honesty left Sam and me stunned and speechless.

We tried everything to get rid of Sam's unrelenting pain, but relief would not come. Not with dozens of medications, including chemotherapy treatments designed to shrink swelling; not with herbs; not with massage; not even with prayer.

I kept telling Sam that there was a light at the end of this dark, scary tunnel. Convincing him became my daily mission. Convincing myself was another matter altogether. I was filled with guilt. What was I thinking, taking my young, healthy son to such a precarious place? I retraced every day of our journey to Benin, trying to track down the culprit in my mind. Had there been bacteria in the food? Had a curse been aimed our way when we visited Ouidah, where voodoo was born and is still practiced with an evangelical zeal? The nagging guilt and the useless theorizing kept me up nights. It shook me to my core.

I will always be deeply grateful for David Bryan, the head of New Roads, Sam's school, who wheeled Sam into his cramped office and assured him that he must return to class. What he said to Sam was enough to send us both on the road to recovery. David reminded him, "The school would not be the same without you, Sam. We all need you here. Even if your pain and meds cloud your concentration, we still want you to come to school every day. Even if you can't complete your work, you need to be here. Your teachers will understand. Even if you can't make it through the whole day, just to be here for a few hours would be enough to make a positive difference for you and everyone else at the school."

David made sure ramps were installed over bumpy curbs. Ralphie and Shelton, the high school guardian angel security guards, met us every morning to hoist Sam and his clunky wheelchair out of our car and into a new day filled with friends and welcome distractions.

Going back to school gave Sam a glimmer of control, something he'd craved but couldn't seem to regain. Watching him start sophomore year in a wheelchair would seem like nothing to be grateful for, and yet, seeing Sam back at school, away from my constant, watchful, weary gaze was something I was in fact very grateful for.

The healing water at aquatherapy washed over Sam's painful joints and offered the buoyant power he needed to override his weakened spirit. The simple act of standing upright in a shallow pool of ninety-degree water while his physical therapists cheered him on was the first step to getting him back on his feet and on the road to recovery.

No one, not even professional or Olympic athletes, can expect life-long optimum health. And too many people struggle to afford even the most basic level of health care. Many of us have moments, maybe years, where we are at our best, but really, aren't we all seeking health that is *good enough?* Good enough to keep our heart strong, blood pressure and cholesterol manageable. Good enough to stay both physically and mentally flexible. Good enough to make it through another day.

TAKE A DEEPER DIVE

What are you most proud of about your health?

List the top five health assets you possess and how they enhance your life. So often we focus on our deficits, but I believe our strengths deserve a shout-out because they lay the foundation for healthy choices in our lives. Expand this list with ways you commit to good health—daily practices that you feel contribute in a positive way.

How many of your health challenges do you attribute to family genetics?

In writing this chapter, I've had to take an inventory of what physical and mental traits have been passed down to me. Whether by nature or nurture, there are undeniable health challenges my siblings and I all share. What are yours?

As a parent, do you feel you are only as healthy as your unhealthiest child?

This is not a literal statement. Rather, I'm referring to the toll a child's illness takes on a parent's mental health. When my son was very ill, I found it was easy to spiral into sadness and worry even though I knew he was depending on me to be strong. Have you ever found yourself in this situation with your child? How did you move through it?

CHAPTER 7

How Much Is Enough:

MARRIAGE

B y the time you're my age, you've most likely been married at least once or been half of a long-term partnership. Occasionally, I date men in their sixties who have never been married, and naturally, my curiosity is aroused. I try to find imaginative ways to probe deeper without appearing too intrusive or judgmental. Go ahead, call me nosy, but I need to know how a man gets to his sixth decade without ever coupling up. I learned that some were committed caregivers to their parents, with no time for themselves until their parents dearly departed, leaving them the family home along with a last chance for some adventurous adulthood. Or they fell deeply in love with their work and made time for nothing else. I dated a lovely fifty-something man who had been morbidly obese, but once he had gastric bypass surgery and lost more than half his body weight, he gained enough confidence to date.

The saddest reason I've heard for never having married is a horrible childhood. Neglect, abuse, or assault can permanently destroy a person's ability to trust. One man I met who had never married spent the majority of our first date convincing me what a damaged person he was and what a horrible partner he'd be, citing enough lurid examples to make my head spin. It felt like a reverse job interview, with the applicant making his case for why the prospective employer would be crazy to hire him. Job well done. There was no second date.

* * *

When I decided to wed, my only marital models were my parents. They met on a blind date when they were both twenty-seven. My dad was a World War II veteran beginning his career as an electrical engineer in Chicago. My mom was a teacher. Neither had much experience in the romance department, and they claimed to have been virgins when they married. I have no idea if that was true or just a story they agreed to tell us, their nosy kids, but I tend to believe them. My brother was born nine months after their wedding, and my mother fell into what we now know was postpartum depression, and so their marriage started with excruciating challenges that only deepened with time. Three more kids within the next seven years, along with financial strains, and my mother's unpredictable mental illness, created a very volatile household. My dad had no patience with my mother and was often verbally abusive. He often yelled at my mother to "snap out of it" when she was struggling with depression, as if it were that easy. I also remember him telling her to "pull yourself up by your bootstraps," which even to my seven-year-old self seemed utterly ridiculous.

It was painfully obvious that my father was not there for my mother in many ways. I think back to all the times his company moved us around the country, shifting the ground under my mom's feet, dashing any chance she had of deepening a friend or finding a sense of community. The frequent moves exacerbated her mental illness. My parents rarely went out on dates. My dad thought it was a waste of money to pay for a sitter. Even when we were old enough to care for ourselves, I have no memory of them going out or socializing with anyone other than coworkers or family members. The sicker my mom got and the louder

Did your parents' marriage give you enough positive or negative reasons to ponder the merits of marriage?

the yelling got, the more I wanted out of the house. I remember promising myself that if I ever got married and had kids, I wouldn't live in a house with incessant yelling. My childhood had provided more than enough examples of what a poor communication tool anger is. Trying to motivate a child or spouse with fear never brings a desirable outcome.

I married young; many would say too young. I was engaged at eighteen and married at twenty to a handsome fellow student in well-worn, bell-bottom jeans and rock and roll tee shirts who was the chief engineer at my college radio station. I was the late-night DJ, and the night before Valentine's Day, my assigned engineer didn't show up, so I called the chief.

Make no mistake, I was not the coed who headed off to college to find a husband. Getting an education and living an independent life was more than enough reason to move over a hundred miles from home. Finding Mr. Right was the last thing on my mind when I headed to Illinois State University in Normal, Illinois. So imagine my surprise when that call to the chief engineer ended up changing the complete trajectory of my college experience and my entire life.

I am not a spontaneous person. I like to think I am methodical and often consider all angles before making a major life decision. But something just clicked in both my head and my heart on Valentine's Eve, 1976 at the college radio station. After my DJ shift ended, my engineer and I walked back to his apartment and stayed up all night talking. I felt like I had reconnected with an old friend. We were amazed and delighted at all we had in common, surprised to discover that we even attended the same elementary school. The minute I got back to my dorm room, I started missing him. I wanted to know more about him. Our chemistry was undeniable and strong enough to invite him to move into my dorm room within the week. I know, I know, writing about this now sounds crazy to me too. But he was so easy to talk to and fun to be with. We never lived apart for the rest of our days at college. My eighteen-year-old self believed I had enough information to trust my instincts and throw my whole self into this relationship.

Our college cohab felt so natural and easy. We found a comfortable domestic bliss, even when his parents insisted we keep our own apartments. We appeased them by finding apartments across the hall from each other and designated one for studying and one for eating, sleeping, schtupping, and socializing. We got married right after we graduated and stayed married for thirty years, until I had enough and made the decision to end our marriage.

My ex-husband is nothing like my dad. While my dad was dismissive and distracted, my live-in college boyfriend was supportive and encouraging. He attended every one of my theater performances, and we went from working together at the radio station to both being hired at the college television station. I was a news reporter and weather girl. He was a director. We were very social, hosting and attending many parties for both the Theater and the Communications departments. He was an impressive, disciplined student and didn't settle for less than straight As, which was surprising since he also imbibed often. His tall, glass bong was a permanent, aromatic fixture on our coffee table.

During college in the seventies, drinking and doing drugs was nothing out of the ordinary, some might even argue a rite of passage. I was not the heavy, habitual user that he was, one drink or a puff off a joint was enough for me at parties. We were in college during the 1970s, when alcohol and drugs were very much part of the culture. To this day, the smell of beer reminds me of the Illinois State University Tau Kappa Epsilon frat house floor.

Once we both graduated, we got married right away. I was twenty, he was twenty-two. Getting hitched seemed to make perfect sense to our immature selves at the time, although once I had my own family, I prayed my kids would never come to me at that young age and say, "Hey, Mom, I met the person I want to marry," because how could I say, "Nooooo! You're way too young!"

> **What role—if any—did drugs and alcohol play in your courtship? Would you say they were enough of a social lubricant to alter your perception of romance?**

While we chose to marry young, we were smart enough to wait ten years before starting our family. Shortly after we married, we moved into a Chicago lakefront high-rise, and launched headfirst into our respective careers. We were financially stable and by all outward appearances seemed in balance and on course.

When we had our kids, he showed up in all the right ways and was a very present and loving dad. I knew he was still drinking and doing drugs, but he was enough of a 'high-functioning' user that he seemed to be able to compartmentalize his using from his family responsibilities.

I realized our marriage was steadily eroding from the corrosive dishonesty, and I had to face the fact that my life and our family life had become unmanageable. After twenty-five years of marriage, I found his gaslighting untenable, and hearing flat-out lies about his drug use and defensive justifications over his drinking in multiple marriage counseling sessions, made me kick myself for wasting the time and the money. He refused to acknowledge the damage his behavior was causing. He was clearly living in a reality that bore no resemblance to mine.

I never felt so alone than when I shared a bed with my husband during our final years of marriage. How much of his addiction was behavioral or biological is something I will never know or fully understand. We grew further apart and were unable to comfortably socialize together. I had enough of constantly making excuses for his inebriated behavior, to myself, to our kids, and to our friends. The smallest everyday conversation became contentious and confusing. We became a *throuple*. Addiction became the third partner in our marriage. Who was I communicating with? My husband, or the addict/alcoholic? When the lines became imperceptibly blurry, I was hurt, defeated, and exhausted. I had enough.

The Beauty and Wisdom of AND vs. BUT

One of the many valuable tips I learned in couples therapy was replacing the word 'but' with 'and.' I learned that using the word 'but' negates anything that came before it, especially an apology that is intended to heal a hurt feeling. Here are two examples:

I'm sorry I was late for our date, but I lost track of time.

I'm sorry I was late for our date, and I lost track of time.

The word 'but' presents a defense. 'And' accepts responsibility. Think about your daily conversations with others and be more aware of replacing your 'buts' with 'ands.' Being mindful of replacing 'but' with 'and' will yield impressive results in your communication with others.

When I decided to end our thirty-year marriage, our kids were teenagers, and several friends asked why I didn't wait until they were out of the house. I found this question preposterous every time it was asked. I had dedicated more than enough time to making this marriage work. I was done, and I no longer wanted to represent love to our children this way. I did not want them to mistake our marriage for something healthy. The kids knew why I was ending our marriage. We were fed up with his emotional absence, the lying, and the way our house and every article of clothing in our closets constantly reeked of pot. We did an intervention, telling him that our family as he knew it would end if he didn't stop. He angrily went to outpatient rehab where he sawed his wedding ring right off his finger with a clear and defiant statement of independence. Our marriage was over. By risking amputating his own finger, he certainly demonstrated that he too had clearly had enough.

My parents were heartbroken to learn about our split. They loved my husband like a son and were confused about his addiction. They had no previous experience with drug or alcohol use, so I had many conversations with them to help them understand the damage that had been done. I remember in one of these conversations asking my dad what he was thinking when he gave his blessing for us to get engaged when I was only eighteen years old. He gave me a weak smile of resignation and said, "You have always been decisive and committed to any decision you've ever made, including talking your way into kindergarten at four years old. No one has ever been able to talk you out of anything. I knew better than to try."

* * *

The archaic wedding vow, "Do you take this man/woman for better or worse, in sickness and in health, 'til death do you part?" is rarely used in ceremonies these days, and for good reason. I remember silently cringing when our rabbi read this at our marriage ceremony. This sweeping declaration is fraught with enough blind consent to leave way too much interpretation in its wake. How much sickness—in my case, addiction—had me rethinking this vow and understanding that I had had enough to part company, long before death did us part?

Do you believe that marriage is a spiritual bond?

When I decided to end our marriage, no one could accuse me of making a rash, impulsive decision. After all, we had been married for three decades. I tried everything I could think of to keep us together, but I was only half of us: the frustrated, weary half who was out of ideas and tired of all the deception. Once I had enough courage to extinguish the gaslights, I saw everything clearly.

The most commonly reported major contributors to divorce is lack of commitment, infidelity, and arguing. While financial stress wasn't specifically listed, I'm guessing the majority of arguing at the end of marriages have something to do with money. Throughout my marriage, I am not proud to admit that I left the majority of our family's financial management up to my husband. He seemed confidently in charge and I was happily occupied, managing my career, along with the domestic aspects of our family, including the children's education and extracurricular schedules, our home, vacations, and social life. I was relieved not to have to also balance our checkbook and pay the bills.

Of course, in hindsight I can see what a huge mistake this was, and I take full responsibility for remaining blindly ignorant in understanding what percentage of our savings went to his addictions. It's been a well-learned lesson. In the years since we split, I've stayed debt-free and proudly learned how to live within my means, even if it means skipping Taylor Swift, Beyoncé, and Brandi Carlile concerts, reigning in my retail therapy, and lunching on leftovers instead of sushi. Living without debt is one of the many silver linings of my divorce.

● ● ●

Alternatives to Going to Bed Angry

Pretty much every how-to book on making marriages work cautions couples about going to bed angry. Few offer specific suggestions for ways to defuse tension so everyone can calm down and get a good night's sleep. You know by now that I am a comedian, not a marriage counselor, so keep that in mind as you consider my suggestions:

1. In the heat of a bedtime argument, take your clothes off. There is a magic shift of anger once we are naked.
2. Keep your partner's favorite snacks in your nightstand. How can I stay angry when I'm being offered a dark chocolate truffle?
3. Create a mutually agreed-upon, nonsensical phrase that either of you can use to call a timeout. Once this phrase is uttered, the argument must end with a hug or kiss while lying in bed, which will hopefully lead to less anger and more sex.

From conversations in my social circle and with my therapist, I have gathered that the most common divorce "final straws" seem to be infidelity, domestic violence, and substance use. Many divorced people blame their ex rather than themselves for the breakdown of the marriage. I have found that pointing my finger outward is always easier than tackling my own stuff. In the years since my divorce, I have found enough self-awareness to understand the role I played in our marriage, for better and for worse. No one is blameless.

What do you think is a good enough reason to end a marriage?

An April 2021 report released by the US Census Department found that 34.9 percent of all Americans who got divorced in 2020 were age fifty-five or older. So much for the mistaken perception that divorce is more popular amongst entitled, impetuous youth. In truth, divorce rates among millennials and Gen Xers are lower than that of Boomers, partially because of the trend toward waiting longer to marry.

And the winners of this generation's *rethinking marriage* movement? Ladies and gentlemen, the crown and the sash go to Gwyneth Paltrow and Chris Martin. They helped popularize 'conscious uncoupling,' a no-drama approach to separation that protects the children and encourages both sides to avoid pointing fingers. In theory, this sounds lovely but in practicality, unrealistic. Since Gwyneth and Chris were so calm and mature, not to mention one of the most wealthy, talented, and attractive couples on the planet, how could they not find a way to stay coupled? If their marriage didn't stand a chance, what did that say about mine? She's an Academy-award winning actress, for God's sake. Isn't 'no-drama' the antithesis of her profession? If I had no drama in my marriage, chances are I wouldn't have gotten divorced. We were deep in the drama and finger-pointing, so conscious uncoupling was definitely not an option for us. Conscious criticizing, maybe.

* * *

My ears perk up whenever I hear people discussing alternatives to traditional marriage. When I was in Japan, I observed people working horrendously long workdays followed by late-night social drinking with coworkers. I wondered how they maintained their personal relationships or if they even had them. I heard dual-income partners talk about *shumatsukon,* or weekend marriages, which are gaining popularity in Japan. In this arrangement, dual-income couples who have demanding and often opposite work schedules live apart during the week, then give 100 percent to their personal relationships when they are together on the weekends. I'm guessing this is mainly for laser-focused professionals who have a hard time leaving their work at work. Would this arrangement work for you?

Now permit me to climb out on a precarious marital limb here.

I admire open marriages. There, I said it.

I really do. I'm not saying that opening a marriage is right for every couple, but I don't think an infidelity in and of itself is enough reason to divorce. It's certainly an opportunity for self-reflection, but should a family be torn apart over it? I am a big fan of psychologist Ester Perel and her theory about infidelity. She has said, "When you pick a partner, you pick a story, and then you find yourself in a play you never auditioned for. And that is when the narratives clash."

In her 2017 book, *The State of Affairs*, Perel contemplates why people cheat, especially partners in happy relationships. She points out that partners commonly discuss and negotiate essential life choices such as finances, where to live, having children, and even end-of-life wishes, then she examines why the topic of open marriage is so comparatively taboo. It certainly was in mine. If a couple have diverse sex drives, interests, or kinks, can there be a world where these can be explored without threatening their primary relationship? Many gay couples seem to have this in the right perspective. At least that is what I gather listening to my friends, along with Dan Savage's podcast, *Savage Love*, and his ongoing dialogue about being "monogamish."

Can an open marriage be enough of a marriage commitment for you?

* * *

Would I rather be happy or right? I cannot begin to tell you how many times I contemplated this throughout my thirty years of marriage. Marriage becomes exhausting if decisions turn into tribunals multiple times a day. I thought of this when I read about Herbert and Zelmyra

Fisher, who hold the record for the longest marriage ever. According to *Guinness World Records*, they got married in 1924 and lived together for eighty-six years and 290 days until Herbert Fisher died in February 2011. Through all these years, how many times did either of them ask themselves, "Do I want to be happy or right?" Could this have been the secret to their long and, I am hoping, happy marriage? In my view, marriage is not a *fait accompli*; your instincts about the relevance of marriage to your life should matter much more to you than others' expectations about whom, when, or whether you will marry.

I am inspired by many of my friends in decades-long marriages. They seem to have made peace with their differences, and their lines of communication stay open. Their disagreements don't linger or get ugly. The love and respect they share is more than enough to nurture their relationships. These friends fill me with hope that durable marriages are not archaic or unattainable. I am pretty sure I'm not going to get married again, but I remain a hopeful romantic.

TAKE A DEEPER DIVE

Do you think the concept of marriage is outdated?

If your answer is yes, what aspects of marriage do you think are outdated? If your answer is no, elaborate on the aspects of marriage that make sense in your life. Share *your* valuable opinion of marriage in your personal journal or with your trusted tribe.

If you chose to end a marriage, when did you know you'd had enough?

For some, the end of a marriage comes slowly, a gradual realization that life could be less volatile or more loving. For others, a secret revealed or an abrupt change in the daily routine makes it painfully obvious that enough was most certainly, enough. If you have been divorced, what was your moment of clarity?

Do you know many happy, single people? If you are a happy, single person, what's the secret to your happiness?

Living single—the opposite of the partnership of marriage—may be an intentional choice. For me, becoming single happened after a long marriage, but maybe for you or someone you know, being single is a life choice embraced as a grand opportunity to live your fullest life, on your own terms. Write about or discuss the single people you admire, respect, and perhaps envy. If you have chosen a single life, list the benefits of your happy, single life.

CHAPTER 8

How Much Is Enough:

F R I E N D S H I P

I am who I am in no small part because of the love and devotion of my friends. Good friends are intentionally handpicked, like the most prized heirloom from an eclectic stall at the Rose Bowl flea market, relocating with me to each new chapter of my life.

My early experiences with friendship didn't portend such an outcome. We moved a lot when I was a kid. When my dad's company transferred us from city to city, often in the middle of the school year, each new school presented a crop of potential friends that felt like a lifeline, offering a new opportunity to join a club or find a new neighborhood hangout. These friends provided an escape hatch from my transient childhood and a comforting alternative to the high-decibel arguments that often awaited me when I returned home.

As I got older, it got harder to leave friends and start all over. But each batch of new friends helped me acclimate to every new school and city we moved to, introducing me to regional foods and local lingo. Like my friends at my suburban Chicago high school, who encouraged me to fix my *T*s, "Claire, it's 'da Bulls,' not 'The Bulls'!"

Who could have guessed that the shaky skepticism I carried into each new classroom full of strangers would turn out to be the ideal springboard that would fill me with enough confidence and chutzpah as an adult to perform in comedy clubs filled with inebriated audience members, emboldened hecklers, and misogynist management?

As a teenager, hanging out after school at my friends' homes gave me the opportunity to observe family dynamics and customs that were dramatically different than mine. Getting invited over to any friend's house after school meant snacking on foods never found in my own kitchen cupboards. Who knew chips came uniformly stacked in card-board tubes and people only ate a few at a time? At my house, all sizes of bagged snacks were considered single-serving.

Thanks to my high school friend Nancy and her sweet family, this Jewish girl grate-fully plotzed to attend a midnight Mass and deeply appreciated receiv-ing my very own Easter basket filled with fancy chocolate eggs and bun-nies. We had no pets when I was a child, so imagine my delight at visit-ing my friend Erin, who basically lived in an animal shelter. Her par-ents had the biggest hearts and would open their doors to any stray, regardless of age, breed, or infirmity. More than once, I remember being in the car with them when they'd swerve off the side of the road to pick up a stray someone had left behind. Feeding time at Erin's home was quite a production, where countless cats and dogs appeared from every nook and cranny of their home to inhale mounds of wet and dry food piled high on paper plates scattered across the kitchen floor, followed by hours of our cuddles. My mother would always know when I had been hanging out at Erin's. She'd smell the scent of eau de damp dog before I walked through the front door in my fur-flecked, kibble-pocked tee shirt and jeans.

What did you learn from your childhood friendships?

In college, my new friends introduced me to a totally new way of life that included productive study skills, experimental theater, pot brownies, and indie rock. After graduation, the unwavering support of my friends was enough to keep me focused as I launched my career. I found that making friends at work can be challenging. Many people spend more waking hours with coworkers than family, so it only stands to reason that deep friendships will form at work. But the subtle unspo-ken power play of management status or financial inequity can throw a monkey wrench into establishing true friendships.

However, I did meet one of my oldest and dearest friends on the job back in the summer of 1977. Betsy and I were both college interns at the WGN radio and television stations, and technically, this was also my very first job out of college since I had graduated right before I began my role as their public affairs intern. My soon-to-be best friend had also been hired for the same position. There was one desk with one chair in the public affairs office, so we were scheduled for opposite shifts, one working the eight a.m. to two p.m. shift and the other slated for the two p.m. to eight p.m. shift.

The more we got to know each other coming and going, the more we felt a connection, and our shifts began to blur. I can't remember at what point in our internships we ended up literally sharing the same chair in a self-proclaimed midday dual shift, but no one at WGN seemed to mind as we began working together and growing closer as friends. That summer I was planning my fall wedding, and Betsy felt herself falling hard for the man who would become her now husband of forty-two years. We had more than enough to discuss that summer, and the closeness we established became a friendship that has lasted forty-plus years.

I marvel at the fact that those three months in 1977 were the only time in the history of our friendship that we lived in the same city. And yet, despite our geographical distance, we found more than enough opportunities to grow closer and closer over the years. We raised children, launched careers, and comforted each other when my parents and her father passed away. Betsy supported me through my divorce and gave me enough confidence to begin dating again. Now we are hands-on grandparenting together, and our bond is even stronger and sweeter as we remain awestruck that our children now have children.

People often refer to friends as 'Family of Choice.' I did it in my Family chapter, but the more I think about this, the more I feel it sells friends short. Friends aren't like family in any way. They are their own spectacular category of unique love and support. Sure, a potent mix of energy, love, and biology creates a baby, but it was my friend Paula who convinced me to take the leap and get pregnant after ten years of marriage over a seafood salad at a sun-drenched patio table at Butterfield's on Sunset Boulevard in West Hollywood back in 1986.

* * *

I've observed that no one needs friends more than new parents. My parents had no close friends when we were young. Even as a child, I thought that was weird. They really could have used some friends, especially my mom, who was so isolated by her mental illness and her responsibilities caring for us, her rambunctious kids. When your world is turned upside down with a new baby, other sympathetic new parents know all the shorthand in providing the psychic support before being asked. Hand-me-downs are lovingly laundered and sent over, extra baby equipment is outsourced, and nourishing meals magically appear on your doorstep moments before you realize you are hungry.

How do your friendships affect your day-to-day decision-making?

These friends become an absolute, invaluable necessity because you need to be able to trust your kids with someone else when family is unavailable or unable to assist. Just knowing another new parent has your unlaundered, ragged, nightgown-ed back should the need arise is enough to get you through the tough days that follow sleepless nights. These friends help you become better people who raise better people, and often these friendships last a lifetime, long after your children are grown and launched.

Friends made through common anguish and pain sounds like the worst way to come together, but for me, it has been one of the most rewarding. When my marriage ended because of my husband's addictions, I joined Al-Anon, and through the Twelve Step community, I discovered a shorthand to intimacy through fellowship. The people I meet in these meetings have no time for small talk. They are in crisis and are seeking relief. By cutting out frivolity and getting to the heart of the matter, we find out quickly if we have enough in common to form deep connections. I learn so much about myself and my capacity to love and care for others in the process. Many people think it takes years to grow close to a friend, but I learned that conversations shared in just one meeting can be enough to break down walls of resistance and establish a tight bond that can last decades.

* * *

Pre-pandemic, life in Los Angeles was filled with party invitations, a vibrant comedy community, long beach walks, and comfy dinners in familiar neighborhood haunts.

When I moved to New York from Los Angeles, I left behind my diverse circle of friends. Saying good-bye to them was one of the toughest parts of the move. I am an extrovert, and I struggled with the isolation and the loneliness when I first moved here. It felt daunting, especially during a pandemic, to attempt to build a whole new social community. I told myself that making even one new friend would be enough. I joined every local social group I could find to meet people, but most groups were meeting virtually. Meeting people for the first time via Zoom felt like a mash-up between *Hollywood Squares* and a bizarre, virtual, speed dating experiment. It just didn't work for me.

After the move, I was forced to do a social inventory of sorts and reflect on just how many friends are enough for me to feel a sense of belonging in the world. Once I unpacked my boxes and settled into the quiet din of my new home, I wondered, *Will my West Coast friends venture east to visit? How will we stay close and in touch? How do I make new friends in my sixties when the rules of engagement have changed so drastically?*

Not to get all Mr. Rogers on you here, but I often find myself involuntarily singing, "Would you be mine? Could you be mine? Won't you be my new friend?" as I pass interesting people on my morning walk through Prospect Park. My heart is always open to new friendships. And while I cherish my friendships that span decades, for me, new friends can be just as impactful and life-changing. New friends with no memory of my past escapades accept me for who I am today, providing a fresh start and new perspectives that friendships imprinted with history can't offer. Think of second or third marriages, but without the marital mishigas. No negotiations about chores, finances, or fidelity. That's the gift of a new, middle-life friend. Sometimes a shared love of weekday morning movie matinees can be enough to launch an invigorating and enduring, nonjudgmental, popcorn-for-breakfast kind of friendship.

Here in New York, I'm grateful to have Nancy, my dear friend from my Chicago days, who lives just across the river in New Jersey. She has lovingly helped me to find my East Coast social footing. "No pressure," I told her as soon as I moved east, "but you are my only friend here in New York." For now, time with Nancy is enough to connect me with my past and give me confidence to seek out new East Coast friendships.

What was the most unexpected place you found a close friend?

In this new, post-pandemic chapter of life, I regularly survey my diminished social calendar, and read *The New Yorker* in search of enticing new restaurants, museum exhibits, and theater openings, all hopeful terrain for making new friends in a town where many people my age appear to have partners, enough friends, homes and social lives in multiple cities, and don't appear to be motivated to widen their circle.

Despite having been uprooted so often in my life, I am heartened by the knowledge that several of my current friendships span over four decades. I still have dear friends from high school, college, and my early career days. Each of these friends offers a touching reminder of how far we've come on our respective journeys. When I meet adults my age who have been friends since childhood, I marvel at such tenacious ties and am eager to learn the secrets to their loving longevity.

* * *

I feel so lucky to have friends of many ages and backgrounds. Some of my friends are closer to my kids' ages, and some are decades older than me. I am especially grateful for my older girlfriends. What a valuable, life-altering perspective I have on growing older as a result of watching these women age so gracefully, purposefully, and with such vibrancy, blowing all negative misconceptions of aging women out the window. These gorgeous, sexy, successful women have given me enough perspective to form a much brighter outlook on my future—not to mention the thousands of dollars I have saved on hair dye, Botox, and futile plastic surgery.

As a parent of adult children, I've appreciated the opportunity to get to know my kids' close friends. I love watching how many of my daughter's thirty-something friends are getting pregnant and having their babies together, swapping onesies and stretch-mark salves. My son formed a passionate group of movie-loving friends who created a Scorsese Zoom School during the pandemic and virtually screened close to a dozen of his best films with spirited discussions following each one.

Watching my five-year-old granddaughter, Natalie, make friends is a wonder. She is completely at ease and makes new friends like it's the most natural thing in the world and something she's done a million times. It's like watching Billy Joel sing "Piano Man" in 2023. My granddaughter is very outgoing and has no problem approaching kids she has never met on the playground and befriending them, regardless of their age. Engagement with just one new pal is enough. If others snub her, Natalie just moves on without a second thought while I tend to my own triggered heart.

When my granddaughter recently inquired about the lines on my face and that of her much, much younger momma, I told her they are laugh lines, and if she is lucky enough to live a happy life like her momma and me, where you get to have lots of fun, she too will get to have faces like ours. She nodded in agreement. I love how five-year-olds haven't been around long enough to be cynical.

Friendship is often seen as "less than" in comparison to romantic love. Why does the phrase *just friends* become the kiss of death in a romantic relationship? Putting the word *just* in front of *friends* is like putting *sugar-free* in front of *chocolate* or *three-karat* in front of *gold*. It just takes some of the wonder and sparkle out of the meaning. But doesn't this sell friendship short? Shouldn't *friend* be a badge of honor, enough of a treasured distinction bestowed on someone who really matters in your life?

* * *

I would like to weigh in on the debate about the ability to have deep, platonic friendships with the opposite sex. I've had extremely close friendships with men that have never turned flirtatious, and no, I am not referring to my gay male friends whom I also love very much.

Case in point: my friend David. He and I have been tight since college. He and his then wife were both close friends of mine. When they split up, she was uncomfortable with my unwillingness to also split up with David. I felt more confident about staying friends with both of them than she did, so she cut me loose. David and I got closer and closer over the forty-plus years since we graduated, and he remains one of my dearest friends. There has never been any awkwardness between us. His current wife is accepting of our friendship and also knows how much I love and honor their marriage. David and I are honest and open in a way that is unique in no small part because we are of the opposite sex. His insights into the male psyche have been invaluable to me during my post-divorce dating detours. I've sought his counsel when things

Do you have close platonic friends of the opposite sex?

went south and his male perspective was just what I needed to calm down and move on. When I go on and on about a lost love, imagining any number of reasons why things went kaput, David shares helpful insights, such as, "No, Claire, that's not what he was thinking. What he was most likely thinking in that moment was, 'I wonder if there is any leftover pizza in the fridge.'" I cannot say enough about the positive impact a platonic friend of the opposite sex will have in your life. Get one. Be one.

* * *

Something rarely discussed is the awkwardness involved in ending a friendship. Friends are forever, until they're not, and very few guides offer advice for navigating nonromantic break-ups. They are unique in that they don't involve dividing property and there are no child custody agreements or spousal support haggling. Sometimes a friendship ends with a big accusatory blowout, but more often than not, you just stop talking to each other and drift apart like a ship that breaks up at sea after a crushing storm. One respectful post-break-up conversation would be enough to provide some comfort and closure, but for some mysterious reason, that is rarely offered.

And let's be honest, it's not always sad to end a friendship. Sometimes it's a relief. I urge you not to judge yourself for not feeling worse that a friendship has ended. Some friendships, like cartons of milk, have an expiration date. It does you no good to ingest the sourness that comes with both. I do my best to process broken friendships by taking responsibility for whatever my role was in the split, then doing what I can to move forward without regret.

What are your reasons for ending a friendship?

You're Never Too Old to Make New Friends

In my attempt to make new friends in my sixties in a brand new city, I've expanded my approach towards meeting new people. Here are a few paths to follow:

1. Online. Virtual friends are people too. Bumble, the popular dating app, has a friendship category. Reddit group threads are a great way to connect with like-minded smarties like yourself. Meetup.com began in New York City post-9/11 when people were desperate to build community. Anyone can form a meet-up for any reason and you are welcome to join. Every hobby from stamp collecting to crocheting, every sport from rock climbing to chair yoga, and every social activity from Scrabble to speed dating has a Meetup.

2. Volunteering. Volunteer for a cause you are passionate about, and chances are there are other passionate people who will warmly greet you and appreciate your service. Imagine the great conversations you could have while grooming dogs at the local shelter, organizing materials for a historical society, or mulching flowerbeds at your grandchildren's school.

3. Living arrangements designed for your life stage. Some neighborhoods have a lot of young families. Other neighborhoods (or condos or retirement communities), are implicitly or explicitly oriented toward empty nesters. If you're deciding where to live, consider the social opportunities available as well as interior design and square footage. After my mom died, my dad moved to an independent living community. I was pleased to

see how he made friends through the many activities he attended there. The daily 7:30 a.m. poker games gave him a reason to get out of bed in the morning and offered valuable social continuity. He never cared if he won his poker games. For him, the companionship that took place around the table was enough.

Friends are a stress valve, a place to vent, a portal of compassionate care. When I suffer a loss, my friends swoop in like a SWAT team, ready to protect and defend me from dashed hopes, a broken heart, hurt feelings, or a bad haircut. Just one conversation in which I feel truly heard by a friend can be enough to begin the healing process. But it's not just about sharing burdens. When something good happens, it gets bigger and better when I share the news with a friend.

At this stage of my life, I'm dusting off my post-pandemic self, practicing my New York state of mind, and learning how to re-establish a social life. I'm putting more effort into my appearance, even if I'm just headed to the market. Hey, you never know who you might meet squeezing a grapefruit, gawking at a tomahawk steak, or balancing a bouquet of sunflowers at the checkout counter. And I am easing in to my new approach of quality vs quantity of friends. Thanks to technology, I've been able to maintain my precious West Coast friendships. A few FaceTimes a week are enough to stay current and feel connected.

> **Are you more inclined to reach out to friends when good things happen or when bad things happen?**

I look forward to getting to know the East Coast friends I haven't met yet. For now, my imagined social life with them is enough. They'll take me to their favorite Manhattan hot spots, and we'll attend numerous Broadway plays together. They'll invite me to their summer homes in the Berkshires, Martha's Vineyard, and the Hamptons. We'll play hours of Bananagrams and laugh about our old love lives. We'll happily stand in line together at film festivals to see three or four screenings in a day. We'll share vegetables from our gardens and swap grandparenting foibles. We'll host regular pot luck dinner parties, widening our friendship circles, and we will grow old together, grateful to be sharing this second half of our lives.

TAKE A DEEPER DIVE

Who is your oldest friend and what is your secret to maintaining that friendship?

Since moving to Brooklyn two years ago, I've attempted a version of platonic speed dating to find new friends. However, no one will replace the friends with whom I have a history that continues to deepen with time: my high school friends Doug and Nancy, along with my college chums David, Sue, and Marla, who are still near and dear. Long, deep friendships are definitely a gift of age. Who are your oldest friends? What's the secret to your long-term friendships?

At what points in your life did you form your closest friendship(s)?

How do you define a close friend? Is it history? Shared interests? Serendipity? Reflect on the times in your life you met someone and just knew they'd be your friend for life. List life passages where friendships seemed to develop organically.

***Do your friendships enhance or challenge your
relationship with your primary partner?***

If you are coupled up, do you have friends who are yours
and yours alone as well as mutual friends? Is there jealousy? Write about the role your friendships play in your
relationship. Are they an enhancement, an escape hatch,
or a combination of both?

CHAPTER 9

How Much Is Enough:

F O O D

My life revolves around food, and my relationship to food is complex and deeply personal. For me there can never be enough perfect bites, comfort foods, or decadent dinner parties with friends. As I dive deep into my feelings about food in this chapter, I invite you to pull up a seat at my table, unfold your napkin, and reflect on your own gastronomic history and the way you approach the concept of *enough* food.

For me, my first visit to The French Laundry in Yountville, California, holds an everlasting sense memory. I can close my eyes and remember the first and last bite of Chef Thomas Keller's "Oysters & Pearls," which utterly seduced me over twenty years ago. This porcelain cup of creamy tapioca custard where plump Malpeque oysters nestle under a quenelle of caviar makes no sense on paper, but oh, in my mouth it became a gastronomical sensation that remains in my dreams decades later. This singular dish is a great example of a time when enough is actually enough. When the dish is set in front of me, this petite, perfectly portioned stunner beckons me to go in for a taste with the accompanying mother-of-pearl spoon. The first bite is positively swoonworthy. As the tiny caviar eggs pop between my teeth and the silky custard and oyster slide down my throat, my bites get smaller and smaller, more studied,

Is there a meal that holds an indelible memory for you?

until I sadly realize I am at my final spoonful. Chef Keller shows how masterful he is at portioning. It is, of course, instinctual to want more and more of this creation, but eating more would diminish how incredibly special this dish truly is. Leaving me wanting more is genius, especially since the dish is served at the beginning of an extensive multicourse prix fixe menu that costs as much as my plane ticket to get there.

I often plan vacations around highly coveted dinner reservations, and I know I'm not the only one. Travel professionals often know of opportunities to secure dinner reservations at Michelin-starred restaurants along with flight and hotel bookings. Go ahead and spend all your money on souvenir tchotchkes if you need something tangible to prove you went on vacation, but for me at this point in my life, the memory of a perfectly plated meal in a beautiful setting is enough.

One of my favorite food-focused vacations was taking my son and daughter to Paris on a pastry crawl. We mapped out all the patisseries we wanted to visit, making sure they were spread out across the city so our consumption would be justified by all the walking we'd be doing. We made a pact that we would each order something different at each stop and offer each other bites so we'd have a dazzling array of sweet treats to sample. Delicate pastel macarons, chocolate-lacquered eclairs, and flaky striped mille-feuille were just a few of our decadent purchases. We made sure we took the time to admire the elegant display cases, which were grand enough to display jewelry, and the glittering decor lit by crystal chandeliers. Each pastry was nestled in a fluted paper cup and wrapped in ornate packaging tied with a satin ribbon. The sight of the Eiffel Tower may be enough for other tourists, but for me and my kids, Paris memories will always include pastry.

Don't get the wrong idea, I am by no means an elitist eater. Many people go to Las Vegas to gamble. Others go for the shows. I go to eat. The cuisine ranges from refined to ridiculous. Somewhere in the middle are the all-you-can-eat buffets, and toward the ridiculous end is an honest-to-God real restaurant called Heart Attack Grill, where customers have literally been carried off on stretchers after consuming one of their gargantuan entrees. Las Vegas deserves its reputation of "enough is never enough" when it comes to food. And believe me, I stand in judgment of no one. Nowhere else but Vegas would I consider filling my plate with an odds-and-ends assortment of crab legs, shrimp, pâté, satay, dumplings, spareribs, stuffed mushrooms, and pigs in a blanket. And that's just the first plate—the appetizers.

* * *

Pasta ranks high on my list of favorite foods. When I was a child, my mother would serve us heaping bowls of "macaroni" instead of pasta because it wasn't called pasta when I was growing up. Macaroni was inexpensive, it was filling, and not one kid in my family ever complained when a bowlful was set in front of them. If my mom felt fancy, she'd break out the metallic green canister of powdered "cheese" and sprinkle some on our bowls before serving. If you would have told the young, macaroni-loving me that one day I would work in the pasta capital of the world, I would never have believed you.

What's your comfort food that you can never get enough of?

What's the menu and location of your fantasy meal?

In 2018, I had the very good fortune to work in Italy, co-hosting culinary immersion programs that combine all my favorite things: travel, meeting new people, and of course, food. The guests who are attracted to culinary travel are generally wonderful, open-minded people who wish to learn about a culture one dish at a time. It really is an ideal way to fully immerse oneself in a country's history, traditions, and of course cuisine. In Italy, food is prepared directly from what grows nearby, often in family backyard gardens. Tomatoes taste different there: dense, yet juicy, the base for the best sauces. Olives are picked by hand from groves that were planted several generations ago. *Cinghiale*—wild boars that roam the Tuscan countryside decimating private property like rototillers—are hunted and happily consumed by vengeful farmers. Most families here, regardless of acreage, have a vineyard where grapes are grown for wine or balsamic vinegar.

Italians are the most hospitable farm-to-table mavens. Our meals together spanned hours and inspired relaxed conversation that brought everyone closer and made us feel instantly connected. One bowl of freshly made pasta was enough for a day, but it also left us longing for one tomorrow, and another the day after that. By the end of each week, friendships were formed, our love for all things Italian had grown deeper, and we no longer craved a daily dose of pasta.

* * *

Today, as I gaze down at my curvy, sixty-six-year-old, always-up-for-a-nosh self, it's hard to believe that I rarely thought about food for the first fifteen years of my life. Back then, I ate only when prompted, and a breakfast bowl of Cap'n Crunch was enough to propel me until dinner. I was the super-skinny tall kid—you know, that girl in your grade school whose clothes never really fit right. My arms were too long for my sweaters, and my pants were too short for my legs. It was like dressing a scarecrow. I was placed in the back row in class pictures.

Being a picky eater was a luxury none of my siblings and I had the good sense to adopt. My mom worked with a tight food budget to feed a family of six. Food was served simply and routinely. Her recipe rotation consisted of about five or six standard dishes, with which I quickly grew bored. How much roast chicken, meatloaf, overcooked hamburgers, and cabbage casserole can a kid endure? The only tempting foods in our house were haphazardly hidden on high shelves by my overweight, overwhelmed mother, who stashed Girl Scout cookies, Pringles, and Entenmann's coffee cakes the way an alcoholic hides liquor bottles from loved ones' anxious inquisitions. In hindsight, I now realize these furtive, favorite foods were often just enough to help my mother find her footing and make it through a stressful day.

My interest in cooking and eating more adventurous fare peaked in college, when I worked in restaurants and at a kitchen supply store called The Garlic Press, a name that amazed me. How do you press powder out of a jar? This Midwest college coed had never seen a bulb of fresh garlic in her life. When the shop owner did an in-store fresh pesto, pasta cooking demo, I marveled at the knobby bulbs and loved the way my hands smelled as I peeled the papery jackets off the smooth cloves.

Multicultural food remained an exotic mystery until I was out on my own. The closest thing to international cuisine I ate as a child was Chun King in a can and Gino's pizza rolls. I vowed that when I became a parent, my family would travel the world via our dinner plates. And sure enough, as soon as my two children could eat solid food, we drove to Los Angeles' vibrant Chinatown to sample a wide range of cuisines very different from my home cooking. Dim sum became our favorite Sunday ritual in the way many families frequented IHOP. One potsticker was enough to convert my children to the wonderful multifaceted world of Asian cuisine. Our friends and their families would often join us at our favorite Chinatown dim sum banquet hall. We'd be seated around the huge round table with a lazy Susan that groaned under towers of bamboo steamers and multilayered metal tins of Har Gow, Shui Mai, and fragrant, warm sesame balls filled with red bean paste. My kids would gather under the table and giggle as we passed dumplings down into their eager, open hands. One of my favorite dim sum memories includes my son, Sam, then five, who popped up excitedly and announced to everyone, "Look what I found right under this table! Free gum!"

Travel the World from Your Dinner Plate

Too many families get stuck in a culinary rut, cooking the same rotation of meals. Explore the world by committing to serve one new international meal a week, either via takeout from your local restaurants, ordering from Goldbelly, or with simple recipes you can find online. Don't know where to begin? Afraid of spices your palate is unfamiliar with? Here are some palate-pleasing suggestions that can serve as a gateway intro to international deliciousness:

1. Chicken tikka masala with naan bread is simple Indian comfort food without too many spices.
2. Cacio e pepe is basically grown-up mac and cheese, Italian style. It's so easy to make: just pasta and grated cheese topped with a grind of cracked pepper.
3. Assorted tapas are little one-bite wonders that serve as a great intro to Spanish cuisine.
4. Chirashi bowls consist of assorted sliced fish on a bed of rice, giving you a chance to sample different characteristically Japanese tastes and textures.
5. Fufu, popular in West Africa, is a highly nutritious dish made of pounded yam, eaten by hand and served with a piquant peanut sauce.

I am proud of many things as a parent, but the fact that my kids grew up to be great cooks really bursts my buttons. Family meals were important, and while we did eat out a lot when they were growing up, cooking together was precious time spent learning and nourishing. I respected their individual palates and preferences, even if meant daily dollops of mac and cheese.

One night when Sam was eight years old, I set a platter of barbecue ribs in the center of the dinner table. Sam stared at them forlornly, looked up at me, and said, "I love animals too much to eat them." He didn't take another bite of meat for the next nine years. As he and his palate matured, he grew more and more interested in innovative culinary pursuits and decided to return to his previous life as an omnivore.

As a parent, did you worry that your kids didn't eat enough?

I loved when my kids' friends asked if they could stay for dinner, and sleepovers offered bonus opportunities to feed them. Could there ever be enough snacks in the house to feed a ravenous rock band composed of five fourteen-year-olds? This is not a trick question. The answer is a resounding NO. Like magic, entire Costco-sized boxes of Healthy Choice frozen fudge bars would disappear faster than Houdini could escape from his straitjacket.

* * *

How do you know when you've eaten enough? Is satiety more physical or emotional for you?

I was fed very few fresh vegetables growing up. Limp, overcooked vegetables were a pale, unappetizing facsimile that appeared often on my family's dinner plates. We had no access to farmers' markets, and canned veggies were really all my parents could afford. Occasional salads were as close to fresh as we got. They were composed of shredded iceberg lettuce, a few slices of cucumber or carrots, and a flavorless slice of supermarket tomato doused with a glug of equal parts ketchup and mayonnaise.

I fell in love with fresh vegetables as an adult, so I was determined to give my children better options than I'd had. When the kids were three and six years old, I jackhammered the end of our driveway in Burbank, California, and created a four-foot by six-foot raised garden plot. Growing vegetables with my kids was an activity I really looked forward to, and our garden inspired many conversations about the beauty and providence of fresh food. I loved how excited they got watching everything grow in our garden. We learned all about patience as we stared at the soil every day, eagerly watching for the plants to peek out of the soil and begin languidly uncurling their leaves toward the sunlight. As the plants grew, the kids and their friends measured their height against stalks of corn and dug deep in the soft soil for carrots and potatoes. My kids plucked bright green pods off the vines, split them open, and eagerly popped raw peas into their mouths.

Container Gardening

For those who don't have space for a garden bed, container gardening is an ideal solution to grow seasonal herbs, florals, and vegetables. Think beyond your windowsill. Unexpected spots for container gardening include:

1. Fire escapes. In New York, residents of older buildings are lucky enough to have outdoor garden space on the landings of their sturdy metal fire escape stairs.

2. Your front stoop. Greet your guests with a front entrance flanked with large potted herb topiary, miniature lemon trees, or overflowing bowls of edible flowers. Visit your local garden shop to find out what grows best in your region.

3. Unexpected containers. Anything can become a home to a plant. Google Ron Finley, "The Gangsta Gardener," for further inspiration. He teaches people how to plant beautiful, purposeful gardens in the most unexpected places in recycled vessels with the most stunning results.

Raising kids in Southern California provided a long and bountiful season. They took ownership over their harvest, even carving their names into the tiny baby zucchinis, watching their names expand as the squash grew. Sam's zucchini grew the length and width of a baseball bat before he agreed to cut it off its vine. Imagine my pride when backyard playdates with classmates often included spontaneous snacking on veggies right off their vines. The warm, plucked tomatoes sent home with friends were enough to inspire many to plant their own gardens, which endeared me to their parents, who had all but given up getting their kids to eat veggies.

These days I'm growing food with my five-year-old granddaughter, Natalie, in our Brooklyn backyard. The seasons are shorter and our raised beds are frequented by hungry critters that appear to thrive on fresh salad, munching our lettuce right down to their roots. Natalie squeals with delight over the wriggly earthworms, the fluttering ladybugs who perch on her shoulder, and the resilient roly-polies she tosses excitedly from one muddy hand to the other. She loves the feel of the warm, damp soil between her toes. Who knew gardening with bare feet could be so sweet?

* * *

I continue to be inspired as a backyard gardener thanks to chefs like Alice Waters, who has taken her passion for cooking out of her kitchen and into schools everywhere. How grateful I am that there are over five thousand Edible Schoolyard projects around the world thanks to the vision of Chef Waters. She and other passionate educators have made it their life mission to help students connect with food, nature, science, nutrition, and, most importantly, each other through fresh-picked school lunches.

Do you remember your school lunches? The rabid trading that took place? The status symbol lunch boxes that served as a gateway to designer hand-bags? The important social intel that was exchanged between bites of bologna sandwiches? Just the antic-ipation of lunch period was enough to get me through my most boring, dreaded math classes, questioning the relevance of the Pythagorean theorem to my preteen life as I counted the minutes until I could crack open my turquoise Beatles lunch box and inhale the contents.

Were your school lunches sustenance enough to get you through the school day?

In New York, every child who attends public school gets free break-fast and lunch. This is a welcome relief for the parents on a tight budget struggling to feed their families three meals a day. And also for those who are just plain sick of packing lunches and have given up the illusion of being able to control what their children eat while at school. I'm sure I'm not the only one who has spotted multiple school lunchroom trash cans filled to the brim with whole fresh fruit and Ziplock bags filled with artfully cut carrot and celery sticks. Local juice shops would have a field day upcycling these farm-fresh castoffs.

In February 2022, twelve years and after the Covid pandemic, the US

Department of Agriculture announced updates to school nutritional standards that include more whole grains and less sodium in processed foods. Many parents say that these updates are helpful but not nearly enough. Few would disagree that fresh, healthy, unprocessed school meals matter to our children, especially for the one in eight children in America who live in households without consistent access to adequate food.

Writing about my school lunches has me thinking about an array of sense memories associated with food. A whiff of the salty, heady smoke of a popcorn popper immediately transports me to the first time I visited a movie theater with my mother. I was five years old when she took me to see *West Side Story,* and that was the first time I ever tasted popcorn. I can also be transported back to my childhood through the scent of butane igniting a charcoal briquette. Any food sizzling and crackling over flames is enough to invoke memories of annual family summer trips to Camp Tuolumne in Yosemite, California.

Often, certain foods hold indelible memories of time spent with my loved ones. One bite of a dill pickle transports me back fifty-five years to the large, wood-slatted pickle barrel at the Main Street concession stand at Disneyland. I'm back at the park with my dad, who always had to start our day at Disneyland eating a pickle and wearing the same cap, which was embroidered with the words, "I'm never growing up," in a childlike font.

Do you have a happy childhood memory that involves food?

* * *

I really love to cook. I love to entertain, and for me, feeding people is a primary love language. When friends say, "Don't fuss, we can order out," I smile and shake my head with pity. Clearly, they don't understand the joy I derive from menu planning, shopping, prepping, cooking, serving, and watching loved ones enjoy my food. As I roll out fresh pasta, deeply inhale the aromas of a simmering Bolognese, and pull a crusty loaf of sourdough out of the oven, I count the minutes until I can welcome friends and family and share what I've cooked. One successfully executed dinner party is enough to carry me through an entire week with happy, obsessive reminiscing of each course.

Seven years ago, I fell in love with a chef. Living together was a fascinating study of the sensuality of food. He was one of the original rock star New York chefs, respected and renowned for the food he made and the company he kept. His food was sublime. Cooking for me in our kitchen was an act of seduction, and boy, did he know it. I would perch on a nearby stool, quietly watching him whisper an apology to a live lobster he was about to submerge in a giant, steamy pot. He'd pivot to stir a lemony beurre blanc sauce, then slide a silky spoonful into my mouth for me to savor. Then he plated, sometimes with tweezers, slowly building the anticipation until we sat together at the table I had lit with candles and set with care. There was no need to dine out with my chef. Eating a meal he prepared for us at home was enough of a treat—and much closer to the bedroom, the ideal location for dessert.

Do you consider yourself a passionate eater? A restrictive eater?

* * *

Restrictive eaters come in a variety of proclivities. I have friends who are lifelong vegans, and while I do believe they are definitely healthier than me, I'm not convinced they are having as much fun. I'm also befuddled by people who hop from one fad diet to another and never seem happy with their results. When a ten-pound weight loss isn't enough, another food group is cut out, and then another, until the dieter grows frustrated, irritable, and, I'm guessing, hungry. And a sad truth was reported in a study by Marschall S. Runge, MD, Dean of the University of Michigan Medical School: 90 percent of people who lose a large amount of weight eventually regain almost all of it.

I have my own daily dance with food because I am medically and socially classified as overweight. I could blame genetics, as both of my parents struggled with their weight most of their adult lives, but I also readily admit my role in my expanding waistline. I briefly flirted with getting gastric surgery after decades of being overweight, but questions the gastric departmental psychologist asked really stuck with me and ultimately changed my mind about surgery. She said, "Are you happy in your skin? Do you feel joy when you eat? Can you be the ultimate judge of how much you should weigh? Not the media, not the medical charts—*you.* Can your opinion of yourself be enough to love and support you?" Years later, I continue to ponder those questions, making a daily commitment to love myself as I am, stop the Instagram doom-scroll shaming, accentuate the positive, and ban self-deprecating hate speech of any kind.

Every meal I enjoy is a gift. I am reminded of this through my work as a volunteer at God's Love We Deliver in New York City. Volunteers cook and deliver nutritious, medically tailored meals for people too sick to shop or cook for themselves. They also provide ongoing nutrition assessment, education, and counseling, and they even bake and personalize birthday cakes for every client. One shift packing up over a thousand meals for people to consume that very same day is enough to remind me how fortunate I am to be healthy and prosperous enough to shop, prep, and cook my own meals.

Do you struggle with the concept of enough when it comes to food?

As I watched my daughter nurse her baby, I reflected in awe upon women's magical ability to sustain the life we birth through our bodies with our bodies. My granddaughter stared deep into her mother's eyes as she nursed, and I pray that those earliest meals were the first of many meals where she will be able to taste the love.

TAKE A DEEPER DIVE

Do you eat for pleasure, for fuel, or a combination of both?

Write about a typical day of eating for you. Are you someone who plans each meal, or do you eat whatever is fast, easy, and available? If you live with others, does everyone in your home have a similar approach to eating? If no, elaborate on the discord.

What role does cuisine play in your vacation planning?

Do you have a favorite cuisine? Have you ever planned a gastronomic getaway with this cuisine in mind? List favorite vacation bites, meals, and memories that were as delicious as they were picturesque.

Would you say you have a healthy relationship with food? If yes, what or whom do you credit for that healthy relationship?

Many people credit genetics for their eating habits, good and bad. How about you? Who gets the credit for your healthy relationship with food? If there is someone in particular, please explain this person's role in and impact on your life.

CHAPTER 10

How Much Is Enough:

T R A V E L

I am at a point in my life where I am happiest when I'm in that perfect space of having just returned from a trip, basking in the reminiscent glow while actively planning my next getaway. I assure you that I'm not running from anything. I love my day-to-day life and its simple, easy pace. But I can never have enough travel in my life. Travel adrenaline makes me feel truly alive and quenches my thirst for new and different experiences.

But there is another kind of traveler who confounds me: the "I'm up for anything" travelers who won't stray far from their comfort zone. Does this sound familiar? You say you love to travel to new places, and yet you stay in the same hotel chain regardless of the country. Or you rent the exact same house in the exact same place every summer. Maybe you say you love to travel, but you don't like "foreign" food. A hamburger and fries in Rome? Really? You may be willing to head out of town, but you want to remain ensconced in your familiar comforts. This style of travel misses my favorite locale: the unknown. Being somewhere new gets my heart pounding and my curiosity piqued. I arrive in a cute new outfit and a fresh mani-pedi. It feels like the perennial first date, where there is pure upside potential and anything is possible. You don't have to travel far to find yourself. A spontaneous road trip can be enough of a journey to make indelible memories that will change your life.

The Gift of Travel

Travel can be the most mind-bending, life-changing gift you can give or receive. Instead of buying things for loved ones, give them an adventure. An opportunity to travel will be deeply appreciated and make memories that will last a lifetime. Here are a few travel gift ideas:

1. Create a staycation for someone with big commitments and very few vacation days. A guided neighborhood architectural tour or a culinary tour where you get to stop at neighborhood restaurants for tasty bites adds a delicious new outlook on your city.
2. Plan a mystery overnight trip, offering only packing instructions to the gift recipient. You plan the itinerary, pack the picnic, and make the reservations. Create a gift card to present in advance of this getaway that creates even more mystery. Perhaps it includes a hand-drawn treasure map, a recipe, or a sentimental photo that somehow ties into the adventure.
3. Go big. Cash in miles or credit card points to buy a plane ticket for someone who's been aching to visit a loved one. Arrange everything on both ends of the itinerary so all the gift recipient has to do is pack and go.

When my daughter graduated college, my gift to her was a ten-day road trip. Our first stop was Las Vegas. Feeling fortified after an all-you-can-eat buffet and a good night's sleep, we headed out for our wide scenic loop: to Bryce and Zion National Parks, Monument Valley, the Grand Canyon, back through Las Vegas, and then home to Los Angeles. This trip was an excellent example of how the journey can be as memorable as the destination. The natural beauty in each park was magnificent, but the drive that led us to each new location was even more special, filled with meaningful chats, an endless supply of car snacks, raucous laughter, and truck stops with cheesy souvenirs.

This is a gift I wish for every parent because there is never enough time with an adult child. Their lives are their own, and their time is primarily spent reinventing themselves from your dependent child to their own individualized adult. To have my daughter to myself for ten glorious days was perhaps the most selfish gift I've ever given anyone.

I imagine my mother must have felt the same way when she invited me to spend my college junior year spring break with her seeing Broadway plays. We shared a compact roomette on the Amtrak Broadway Limited overnight from Chicago to New York City. We stayed at the St. Regis hotel on Fifth Avenue and saw four plays in five days, including the original productions of *A Chorus Line, Equus,* and *The Wiz.* I had never seen my mother so carefree, so unburdened, and just plain giddy, which was a word no one would ever use to describe her. She loved New York and theater, and I know she loved me. That week was a rare, well-deserved escape from her precarious balancing act as a wife and mother living with bipolar illness. We were just two crazy theater fans, hopping from one show to another and eating New York pizza, hot dogs, and cheesecake between each performance. We couldn't get enough of the city and our time together, making it one of my most cherished memories of my mom.

> What trip have you taken that has stayed with you throughout your entire life? What made it so memorable?

* * *

Travel is as unique as the person planning the trip. In fact, for many, the planning and anticipation of a trip is as exciting as the trip itself. Some trips require months of detailed planning and research. Others are as simple as getting into the car and hitting the road with no particular destination. For those preferring the latter, the journey alone is enough.

One drive that I wish would never end is a cruise up Route One along California's coastline. I cannot get enough of that drive from the Santa Monica beaches, through Ventura County past Montecito (*Hellllo,* Oprah!), hugging the coastline below Hearst Castle, and up to Big Sur, where I always stop to take deep, restorative breaths of the salty ocean air, heavily scented with pine, eucalyptus, and more assorted flora than I can name. I know the song says, "I left my heart in San Francisco," but I feel like I leave a bit of my heart on Route One every time I drive through Big Sur. I slowly navigate this winding stretch of road high above the coastline, under the canopy of towering trees that shower me in dappled sunshine through their tangled branches. I never want to leave Big Sur because I never feel like I've spent enough time there. But I have friends and family I love farther north, so I grab a gooey, pecan-studded brownie from the Big Sur Bakery like a consolation prize and climb back in my car. Monterey and Carmel always make me smile. I imagine the graceful jellyfish in their diaphanous tentacled ball gowns floating in the massive tubes at the Monterey Bay Sea Aquarium. I continue on through Santa Cruz, then San Jose. The garlicky whiff of Gilroy gives me the momentum I need to keep heading north until I stop in San Francisco to visit my friends. I've heard that Route One north of San Francisco is just as scenic, and that drive remains on my bucket list. For now, these 382 miles are enough.

* * *

I am amazed that I find car trips relaxing since family car vacations remain amongst my most unhappy childhood memories. As miserable as I was crammed in the back seat of our station wagon with my three siblings, I now have the maturity and the perspective as a parent to appreciate how stressful and aggravating these trips must have been for my parents. The brown-bag lunches my mother packed for us—bulging with bologna sandwiches, baggies of store brand cookies, and bruised plums that soaked a hole through the bottom of the bag and left our laps sticky—were usually consumed within the first hour of our days-long drive. My dad refused all bathroom requests until he or my mother had to go, forcing us to cross our legs and magically coordinate our bladders. Even my bouts with car sickness weren't enough of a reason for my dad to pull over. Once when I was sitting in the way-way back, completely nauseated, I warned my dad that if he didn't pull over I would be sick all over the seat. Without missing a beat, he opened the automatic rear window from his driver's console and instructed me to just stick my head out the window and upchuck while the car kept moving, which I did, to the disgusted delight of my squealing siblings.

Do past road trips contain enough happy memories to make you want to plan another one?

I'm relieved to report that I grew out of my motion sickness. I love cruises and have enjoyed both working and vacationing at sea. I'm always surprised to see how many people wear the small circular air-sickness patches behind their ears while on board, resembling blown-up balloon humans who could deflate any moment should their patch fly open. They persevere because cruising, even through the pandemic, remains the all-inclusive vacation of choice for travelers around the world.

What childhood travel memory would you prefer never to revisit?

During their fifty-year marriage, Ft. Lauderdale Florida residents Mason and Lee Wachtstetter went on eighty-nine cruises. A week before he died, Mason told his wife to keep cruising, and after his passing she took his parting words quite literally. Lee moved onto a cruise ship full-time, taking over a hundred more cruises, including fifteen world cruises. As of 2020, ninety-three-year-old Lee had been living aboard the *Crystal Serenity* full time for twelve years, the longest anyone has ever taken up permanent residence on a luxury cruise ship. It's a fantasy life for sure: no cooking, cleaning, shopping, or schlepping, with a full staff to anticipate your every need 24/7. It costs approximately 175K a year to live Lee's life at sea. Even if I could justify the expense, the perks wouldn't be enough to make me leave my friends and family, who truly keep me afloat.

* * *

First class is the preferred mode of travel for many, and while I appreciate extra leg room, fine dining, and a comfy bed, I also crave unusual, exotic adventures. My trip to Bali with my friend Paula felt otherworldly. I was craving a dramatic change of scenery. I'd had enough of my suburban life and was feeling the undeniable strain in my marriage. I needed an escape hatch and was excited about visiting a tropical paradise on the other side of the globe. Nothing in Bali resembled home: not the wild monkey forest, nor the nasi goreng rice and egg breakfasts, nor the locals who had a connection with nature unlike any I had ever experienced before.

If you had enough money and time to book a dream vacation, what would be your itinerary?

In advance of the twenty-one hour flight, I read about Bali's culture, religion, and traditions, and I decided that I really wanted to attend a cremation ceremony. Now, this is hardly your typical vacation excursion, but we befriended a village guide who agreed to take us to a cremation processional that was scheduled for later that week. We were told we could join the procession where a recently departed resident's body would be taken to the neighborhood pyre. A celebration of life would take place as his physical body burned. We were instructed to look straight ahead as we walked within the procession so as not to confuse the direction of the spirit, and we were sternly warned not to cry or otherwise express sadness. I will always have joyful memories of this ceremony, not unlike a neighborhood block party back home, that transported a beloved man to his next life and gave his loved ones conscious closure.

I'll always remember the talented wood sculptor in Ubud whose studio was an outdoor gazebo that he shared with a chandelier-sized bee hive. The bees loudly buzzed over his head, and I hesitated to enter the space for fear of getting stung. The sculptor calmly explained that this was the bees' workspace, and he was just a grateful guest. That shift in perspective has always stayed with me.

Solo Travel

Are you hesitant to embark on a solo adventure? I encourage you to check off destinations on your bucket list whether you have a traveling companion or not. There are so many advantages to solo travel, including:

1. Going where and when you want to go. Plan your dream itinerary with no one else's tastes, energy level, or interests in mind.

2. Eating and sleeping on your schedule and no one else's. This is perhaps the ultimate gift you could give yourself—a true declaration of self-care.
3. Boosting your confidence. Travel jitters are normal, but solo travel will fill you with pride and remind you that you are capable and strong.

If solo travel still sounds daunting, join an organized tour group, which offers the best of both worlds: companionship when you want it plus opportunities for solo exploration.

Travel adventures don't have to span the globe, and lack of money shouldn't prevent you from venturing out of your backyard. There is so much to see in the USA. Between business travel and pleasure pursuits, I've been to forty-eight of our fifty states. Hey Wyoming and Montana, I'm coming for you!

I did much of my US travel as a stand-up comedian. I often found myself performing in communities that offered a slice of life very different from my own. It widened my perspective about how socially and culturally diverse this country is. Often I would talk to the audiences after the shows, and in the course of discussions about my tour schedule, I learned that many people never travel very far from home. Many people I met said they had more than enough to do and see in their own communities and had little interest in and even some fear of travel. Hearing this over and over made me wonder how reluctance to travel contributes to the social polarization of our country. Fear of travel becomes a wall that separates us from new experiences and prevents us from discovering how much we have in common despite our differences.

* * *

I went to Havana, Cuba, decades ago on an American cultural visa to attend the International Arts Biennale, a rare opportunity for world-renowned artists to come together and share all forms of creative expression. At the time, Fidel Castro was quite ill, not out in public, but still very much running the country with the help of his brother. They courted limited tourism, but the daily oppression of Cuba's people was impossible to ignore and was very much a part of the Cuban landscape. We had CNN available on our hotel televisions, but the hotel staff would have been fired if anyone caught them watching TV as they serviced the guestrooms. Getting locals alone so they could speak honestly about their life and the current state of affairs in Cuba was a precarious challenge. It certainly gave me pause to appreciate many freedoms I take for granted. My country is far from perfect, but the freedom to write a book from one's own perspective, unfiltered and uncensored, and to share it with others with no government intervention seems like an obvious human right. If you can't travel to oppressed countries, reading about them should give you enough of a perspective not to take freedom for granted.

Do you feel you have traveled enough in your life?

I fondly remember meals at Cuban paladares—small independent family-run eateries where multiple generations serve food and drink in the modest dining rooms of their own homes. The Cuban government passed a law in 1995 allowing the sale of "light foods" from households, and entrepreneurial families embraced this opportunity to earn money and share their family stories. Some spoke candidly to me and painted a stark picture of a difficult life in a country where everyone is required to unconditionally support their government regardless of their own beliefs. They spoke of the challenge of feeling rooted in a country where the only real estate a citizen can own is their cemetery plot. Vibrant art, music, and meals were not enough to conceal the daily challenges Cubans endure.

That trip might not be considered a vacation by many, as it lacked the R & R so many people seek on their getaways, but it was deeply impactful for me and much more interesting than planting my tush on a poolside lounge chair for a week.

* * *

One of my favorite modes of travel is the most obvious, yet rarely considered. I love to travel on foot. As a marathon walker, I've completed 26.2-mile routes in seven cities around the world. From London to Alaska, Los Angeles to New York, marathon walking has given me a unique perspective of seeing neighborhoods from the ground up. Along my routes, I've been invited to family barbecues and lemonade stands, and I've cooled off under more than one refreshing shower from a kindly offered neighborhood hose. I've been moved to tears by cheering children lining the routes to proudly welcome racers to their communities.

What is your favorite mode of transportation?

In London, locals even organized pub crawls along the route, beckoning runners off the route to stop and share a pint. Dressing up in crazy costumes was encouraged and certainly kept the race interesting. I especially loved the four marathoners dressed and bound together as the London Bridge, running lockstep the entire route. By the end of that race I knew I had just experienced a slice of London I could never have seen from atop a double-decker tour bus.

* * *

Working in Italy on and off for the past six years has given me the opportunity to travel throughout one of the most beautiful countries on Earth. It has also literally fed my passion for Italian cuisine, introducing me to new unexpected gastronomic delights, including but not limited to drizzling aged balsamic vinegar instead of chocolate sauce over my ice cream. And why use a pan when I can finish cooking my cacio pepe in an actual wheel of cheese? And yes, tomatoes do taste better in Italy.

I often tell people that Italy is more than a destination; it's a state of mind. The emphasis on family and caring for one another was never more evident than during the pandemic when Italy was one of the first countries to shut down and suffer catastrophic loss of life. Now, as the world recovers and readjusts to a new normal, Italian families maintain the same fiercely loyal, devoted multigenerational bonds they have always had.

For generations of Italians, it's not enough to live with family—they work with them, too, often for decades. And they are consummate hosts. There is always an extended hand, a hug, and enough food to set another place at the table. In Italy, food is love.

Agriturismi—working farms that offer food and lodging like a B&B— have kept many Italian family farms thriving for generations. Opening family farms up to overnight guests offers an intimate glimpse into how self-sufficient families can be. They grow what they eat and serve it on furniture built from trees that grew on their land, which has been in the family for hundreds of years. Staying at an agriturismo adds a deeply personal dimension to the tourist's experience of Italy that checking into a chain hotel can never replicate.

* * *

Most people admit that their perspective on many aspects of their own lives changes for the better after they've traveled somewhere new. They return home with fresh eyes and a deeper appreciation for every aspect of their lives. When my then fifteen-year-old son Sam and I returned from Benin, West Africa, we were both woozy from mentally processing the barrage of indelible images we knew would be with us forever. Every day of our trip we witnessed a level of poverty that was equal parts heart-breaking and eye-opening. Meeting people who live rich, meaningful lives with far fewer material things than I take for granted was sobering and profoundly inspiring.

Has a trip ever changed your life? How?

If you are still skeptical about the life-changing power of travel, permit me to share one additional example. Once we returned home from Benin, I helped my weary teenager carry his bags up to his bedroom. He opened his door and surveyed his room as if he was seeing it for the very first time. After a deep breath, he looked at me and said the words every parent yearns to hear: "Mom, I have too much stuff."

TAKE A DEEPER DIVE

Do you think multigenerational trips can be relaxing for all? If yes, how do you accomplish that?

Share details of your best multigenerational trip. Who was in attendance? What was the itinerary? Who was involved in the planning? What advice would you give to someone contemplating a multigenerational vacation?

What sort of trip would take you outside your comfort zone?

I have found that I learned the most about myself from the trips that posed the greatest challenges. Do you find it enlightening to get out of your comfort zone? Detail the trip that has created the most profound memories. Would you take this trip again?

When has travel served as an escape for you? Were you able to find enough solace to return home with a renewed attitude?

There is nothing like a getaway to give me a deeper appreciation for all I have back home. Do you feel the same? Share the details of your most inspiring escape from your reality.

CHAPTER 11

How Much Is Enough:

WORK

I have nothing but respect for the person who feels content enough to spend an entire lifetime in one job, but that is not how I am built. For as long as I can remember, I've been in a constant state of professional reinvention. My very first job out of college was with the Chicago Public Library Broadcasting Department. It was a great job, creating public affairs programming for local radio and TV stations and providing research for their stellar Chicago investigative reporters. This was in 1978, years before the Internet. We were still knee-deep in the Dewey decimals, squinting at blurry newspapers and magazines on microfiche.

On my first day at the library, I was handed a document that all new city employees received, showing my salary and benefits for the next thirty years. The annual cost of living increases were pre-calculated and had absolutely nothing to do with performance or creativity. Basically, if I didn't murder anyone, I would have this job with this income schedule for my entire career. It occurred to me that there were two ways to approach this information: (1) give thanks and settle in, or (2) see this job as the springboard that would bounce me into a deep pool of endless possibilities. I chose #2.

For me, college was enough of a glimpse into my future to widen my gaze towards a myriad of career options. I was a theater major, and among my college classmates was an insanely talented group of actors who went on to form the Steppenwolf Theatre Company and earn international acclaim in television, film, and on Broadway. When fellow college coeds including Laurie Metcalf, John Malkovich, and Gary Cole understandably knocked me out of contention for every plum role, I decided to expand my degree to include radio, television, and journalism. I figured that if I didn't get steady work as an actor, I would have the skills to create my own opportunities in related entertainment fields, and that's exactly what happened.

After graduation, I worked my day job at the library, then spent my nights in comedy clubs, watching every comic that came through town. I began taking classes, and writing my own stand-up comedy act. After four years at my comfy, safe, secure job at the library, I resigned in a bold—some, including my in-laws, might say irresponsible—leap of faith and began pursuing my comedy career full time. I hosted an open mic on Monday nights at a Houlihan's, a Chicago bar and restaurant that was looking to energize their ho-hum Monday night atmosphere. The very first time I hit their stage as a stand-up comic, I competed with a loud espresso machine at the bar right next to the stage that had the uncanny ability to crank up a loud, hissing, foamy cappuccino just as I was delivering a punchline. Monday nights at Houlihan's were a safe space for young comics to work out new material in front of a kind, encouraging audience (and the espresso maker). The experience gave me some sure footing and a chance to find my voice and style on stage as a comedian. I was committed to being kind, never disparaging toward myself or others on stage. Earning a reputation as a "clean" comedian was enough to set me apart from many other up-and-comers.

> **Did your education provide enough preparation for your chosen profession?**

The Beauty of Reinvention

After decades as a stand-up comedian, I knew it was time for a change. Maybe you are feeling the same way about your current profession. Trust me when I tell you that you're never too young or too old for a professional pivot. The skills you've honed in your current role can be easily reconfigured for a new industry. The pandemic inspired many to rethink their chosen professions, but you don't have to wait for a major societal upheaval to change careers. There are many support systems already in place to help you pivot. A few to consider are:

1. SCORE.org will match you up with a mentor who has already had a successful career in your next dream career.
2. LinkedIn.com offers free seminars and opportunities to network with established professionals. Don't be afraid to learn something new. You may surprise yourself. Message someone who appears to have your dream job and ask thoughtful, focused questions about their professional journey.
3. A career coach can help you retool your resume and reconfigure your current skills for a new professional chapter.

Once I got some good press as a stand-up, comedy became my road to employment. I had found my home as a performer, and the positive reception gave me enough confidence to throw my heart and all my professional energy into comedy. I was invited to join The Second City improv company, and I performed in their tour company while continuing to do stand-up in any venue that would have me. In the course of my quarter-century comedy career, I performed for audiences ranging in size from two to 3,000-plus. Comedy brought me some unexpected work, including a job on HGTV, the last network anyone would expect to launch a comedian from local comedy clubs to national acclaim. I was the first female stand-up to host a series there; it was called *Fantasy Open House.*

Once I had kids, I sought work where I had enough time home as a mom while still earning a living as a comedian. I became one of the first women to establish myself as a warm-up comic for television. The job of a warm-up comic is to keep a studio audience engaged, entertained, and alert for the three to five hours it often takes to shoot a half-hour sitcom. It really was the perfect mom job, keeping me off the road and available for my family during the day. Then at night I would dress up and head to the television studios near my Burbank home. I worked on over sixty-five sitcom series throughout the late '80s and into the '90s, including *Seinfeld, Murphy Brown, Friends,* and *Mad About You.*

> **Do you feel you had enough time with your family as you launched your career? Looking back, what would you have done differently?**

Today, I find my daily life provides more than enough opportunities to tap into my comedy expertise. I will always think like a comedian, whether I am in front of an audience, touring guests through Italy, or cajoling my five-year-old granddaughter. My insatiable curiosity about life , attempting to learn a little about a lot of things, honed through improv training, gives me enough confidence to trust my instincts in all aspects of my life.

* * *

Through comedy I learned firsthand the difference between a job and a career. Many have mused over the differences between the two, but none better than Chris Rock. He eloquently and hilariously explains their differences in his act. He traces his own trajectory from a tenth-grade dropout scrubbing dirty pots and pans at Red Lobster to headlining stadiums as an internationally acclaimed stand-up. He explains that when you have a career, there is never enough time to get things done, but when you have a job, time seems to stand still as you constantly check your watch to see if it's time to go home. He cautions those in his audiences who have careers not to talk about them around people who have jobs. Chris says, "Don't let your happiness make somebody sad."

Why do we do what we do? Sometimes there is no choice. If you are born into a family with a business, there are subtle and often not-so-subtle assumptions and reminders that, someday, you will be running the farm, restaurant, or widget factory. In Italy, the majority of restaurants and cafés are run by multiple generations of families. When I asked one restaurateur why so many Italian families are in the restaurant business, he answered swiftly and succinctly, "Great recipes and cheap labor."

Many jobs are physically demanding and require long hours with low wages, few benefits, and little chance of advancement. People without education or proper documentation find their job options are extremely limited. They are forced to take jobs where they can barely eke out enough money to raise a family. Personal pride and dedication to a job well done may feed the soul, but it's rarely enough to feed children.

How has your family influenced your professional career decisions?

* * *

If you are in business for yourself like I am, you are faced with many unique challenges. For me, the toughest has always been knowing when to stop working. When there's no clock to punch or office to leave, how do you end your workday? As a freelance writer, a significant part of my job is actually looking for my next job. So, how and when do I close shop and say, "I've worked enough today"?

During the pandemic, many people found themselves working remotely. They shed their 'work' clothes, onerous daily commutes, and, most importantly, the preconceived notion that one must leave the house in order to be productive. These months of working from home were a time for reflection. People asked themselves unprecedented questions: *Is going to work enough of a reason to risk my health and safety? Is the old way the only way I can earn a living?"* And, my personal musing: *Is there any reason I have to wear an underwire bra or high heels ever for the rest of my life?* I hope we all learned that time with family is precious (even if exhausting), self-care is essential, and if you are a parent, your kids' teachers deserve renewed respect and admiration.

There is so much chatter about the search for work/life balance. I find this to be a highly personal journey, similar to religion, politics, and dieting. I don't have a clue, nor is it any of my business what your best

If you are self-employed, do you have a ritual to signify the end of your workday?

How did the pandemic change your work/life balance?

work/life balance should look like, but it's certainly worth exploring. I will share that in my fifty years as an earner, my work/life balance has ebbed and flowed. I acted like I was shot out of cannon when I graduated college, full of dreams, ambition, energy, and expectations. I still experience bursts of that youthful exuberance, but it's certainly not the rocket fuel I had for breakfast every day of my twenties.

Over the years I have enjoyed many perks of professional success, but none more gratifying than the ability to be present for my children while still achieving many of my professional goals. The relationship I now have with my adult children is more generous, meaningful, and fulfilling than any paycheck, audience response, or critical review I could have dreamed of in my twenties. Could I have convinced my twenty-year-old self that the sounds of my children's laughter, angst, and drum solos would be enough to satisfy me while my contemporaries booked appearances on *The Tonight Show*, Letterman, and SNL? I doubt it, but it's true.

I'm pretty sure the other thing my twenty-year-old self would have found utterly inconceivable is how many times I have pivoted in my career, from actor and comedian to radio and TV show host, author, motivational speaker, and even children's cooking instructor. After my thirty-year marriage ended, I needed a steady paycheck and health insurance. I accepted a job as a communications director at a preschool to get both, and I shifted my career aspirations to side hustles. Every job I've held has brought me a deeper understanding of myself and my capabilities.

> Knowing what you know today, what work/life advice would you like to give your younger self?

What I do to earn a living and who I am as an independent, self-sustaining human often intersect, but not always. If I represent anything to my children, it's that reinvention is not only possible, it's probable and preferable. Life is full of adventurous career careening. Why not experience all that is possible, including work that takes you out of your comfort zone? The fact that my children currently have careers in companies that did not exist when they were in college should be enough of an indication that career paths are rarely predictable.

If you are very lucky, you are employed by a progressive, family-forward company that offers generous paid maternity leave. When companies acknowledge that their employees are valuable even when they are brand-new, sleep-deprived parents unable to complete a sentence, they build a level of loyalty that gives employees more than enough reason to return to work after their leave. My daughter's employer hired her when she was seven months pregnant with her first child and included six months paid maternity leave in her contract. The day before she went on maternity leave for her second child, they gave her a well-deserved raise and promotion, offering her enough incentive to keep work on her mind between diaper changes. And may I also say a hearty *bravo* to the astute companies that also offer parental leave for fathers and same-sex partners?

In which chapter of your professional life were you the happiest both personally and professionally?

My father worked at Motorola as an electrical engineer for over thirty-two years. Typical of the men of his generation, his identity was very much tied to his profession, and the idea of retirement made him anxious. Who would he be without his job title and responsibilities, not to mention the travel and all the other perks? Could staying home with my mother be enough of a life for him?

Do you believe your employer offers enough benefits and compensation for the work you deliver? If no, what more would you like to receive?

I hope you have come to believe that you are more than enough, independent of your job title or professional responsibilities. I really love every chapter of my colorful patchwork quilt of a career. I look back with gratitude for all I have learned and achieved, and I hope you do too.

TAKE A DEEPER DIVE

Most of us have worked jobs we consider unrelated to our careers. Looking back on your own working life, is there anything a job taught you that your career did not?

I have spent the majority of my working days in my career, but I also had jobs that were essential simply to pay my bills and subsidize my health insurance. Make two columns and title one *Career* and the other *Jobs*. List your relevant work experience under each. Do you have any regrets? Any chapter of your work life you wish you'd done differently?

Whose work/life balance do you admire?

My parents' generation didn't think much about work/life balance, perhaps because marital roles were stricter then and employers were less flexible. I struggle to list contemporaries who appear to have an optimum work/life balance. How about you? List those you admire, along with what they did for a living and how they struck a healthy balance.

*What's your dream job? How closely
does it resemble your actual job?*

This is an opportunity to let you imagination go wild. Describe your dream job, including location, coworkers, salary, benefits, contribution to society, and any other relevant details. Now think about your actual career path. How close has it come to that dream job?

CHAPTER 12

How Much Is Enough:

SUBSTANCES

M any of us struggle with the concept of *enough* when it comes to substances. Broadly defined, substances are drugs, alcohol, and anything else that we use indiscriminately to self-medicate. Of all the things people inhale, inject, or swallow for pleasure, sugar is arguably the one we discover earliest in life. How many five-year-olds offered more Halloween candy would say, "No, I have enough"? Most are able to conquer that struggle with time and maturity, although there are plenty of adults who cannot walk past a candy store without ducking inside, and wouldn't take offense at being called "chocoholic."

I will never forget attending an open AA meeting where an elderly man shared that he had proudly kicked alcohol, heroin, and crack cocaine addictions, but he remained confounded by his struggle with cigarettes. Many smokers have told me they started as teenagers and cannot imagine not smoking despite the ever-mounting evidence that cigarettes will ultimately kill them. When I see people hanging around outside AA meetings chain smoking and chugging coffee, I can't help but wonder: do we all just go through life swapping one substance addiction for another?

I begin my own exploration of how much is enough with cake, because I am crazy about cake and believe cake is a universally loved substance. Heck, how would we celebrate weddings and birthdays without cake? I don't know about you, but if I don't have some cake on my birthday, I don't feel as if I've properly celebrated. But how much cake is enough?

I ask myself this question way too often. I look at an elegantly decorated chocolate layer cake, and my very first thought is, *I could eat that whole dang cake.* I gawk at its symmetrical, multilayered construction, a baker's skill I have never mastered, and the thick, swirly topping of chocolate frosting, my favorite part. I mentally analyze the slice that is served to me: is it too big (never), too small (often), and is the ratio of cake and frosting agreeable to me (rarely)? Welcome to my inner cake critic, super seductive and unflappable. Thank God I utter none of this aloud. I snap myself back to my delectable slice. I slowly cut a corner with the side of my fork and savor the first bite of moist, crumbly cake and buttery frosting. I quickly find myself in a euphoric state of bliss that isn't far from what I imagine heroin addicts feel the second the drug hits their bloodstream.

I have deeply mixed feelings when exploring the concept of enough as it relates to substances. My ex-husband's drug addiction and alcoholism decimated our marriage and fractured our family. And yet, I also believe in the power of psychedelic drugs and their power to heal (more on this shortly). I understand how a cocktail or two can be enough to turn a painfully shy introvert into a comfortable, charismatic conversationalist. I have friends who sleep better at night thanks to CBD-infused gummy bears. I embrace the idea of using substances to alter our mood and calm our anxious energy. In the spirit of understanding how much is enough, I strive for a deeper understanding of the difference between substance use and abuse.

What would you say is your most personally challenging substance?

I'm sure that how much of any substance is considered *enough* depends upon any number of factors, including nature, nurture, social acceptance, and spirituality. For instance, if you have generations of alcoholics hanging off your family tree like overripe fruit, you probably want to pay a little closer attention to your consumption. If your family is from a country like Italy, where wine is served every night with dinner to all family members regardless of age, drinking may be less of an event for you than for someone who grew up in a home where no one drank a drop.

I, and I'm guessing you, don't like it when nagging anxiety infiltrates daily consciousness. Simply put, we are not comfortable with being uncomfortable. So, in order to create a sense of mental calm and stability, most of us will resort to some variety of substance use as an escape from nagging daily challenges. Alice found her Wonderland down a rabbit hole. I often find it at the slick, salty bottom of a bag of Lay's potato chips. You may find it in a deep drag from a cigarette or a joint, a shot of tequila, a prescription medication, or an edible. And yes, many people find a precarious comfort in illegal drugs, self-medicating until they've had enough to quiet the screeching cravings that have rewired their brains.

How much was enough alcohol in your childhood home?

I write without judgment here in addressing the question of what is enough of our chosen substance, curious to understand how quick and easy it can be to strap in and ride that zipline from use to abuse.

The first Step in AA reads, "We admitted we were powerless over alcohol—that our lives had become unmanageable." Sounds simple enough, but to admit you are powerless is to acknowledge that you have crossed over from socially acceptable behavior to inflicting pain on yourself and others. To honestly embrace this first step, there must be a deep, personal understanding of enough actually being enough. The thought might go like this: *I have hurt myself enough. I've had enough time to deeply contemplate my actions and the negative impact they have on my loved ones.*

Spending thirty years married to an addict/alcoholic does not make me an expert, but it did offer a front row seat to the day-in-day-out rituals, routines, and myriad justifications for substance use and abuse. For my ex-husband, using all too often began with prescribed pharmaceuticals in the morning, cocktails and one-hits in the afternoon, followed by an endless happy hour filled with deceit, resulting in unconsciousness in the evenings.

I discovered through Al-Anon meetings that those who abuse substances generally believe they are smarter than others and become skilled at charming, cajoling, and deceiving those closest to them. Their twisted sense of justification turns each day into a deranged Mad Libs game:

I deserve this _____ **because**
substance du jour

my _____ **was so** _____ .
noun   adjective
                                  (stressful, unfair, etc.)

Throughout my marriage, I often reminded myself that we were the lucky ones. After all, no one was being beaten, nothing had been stolen, money was earned, and bills got paid. But my kids and I grew increasingly frustrated with the unpredictable outbursts, toxic anger, chronic dishonesty, and hollow apologies.

When our teenage son came home from school day after day to a house reeking of pot and begged his dad to fess up, his glassy-eyed father would say, "What are you talking about? I'm not smoking pot." Come on, it's not like a high schooler doesn't know the skunk stench of pot. The lying was chronic, insidious, and damaging to our family. And when my ex was unavailable for evening social activities because he had usually passed out by seven-thirty, it was painfully obvious that we had an addict/alcoholic in our family. Unless this was addressed, our family would disintegrate. And indeed it did, after an unsuccessful intervention, outpatient rehab, and way too many lies.

* * *

I am equal parts fascinated and challenged by Michael Pollan's book *How to Change Your Mind: What the New Science of Psychedelics Teaches Us About Consciousness, Dying, Addiction, Depression, and Transcendence.*

I watched his Netflix documentary series by the same name, where Pollan interviews people living with cancer, depression, and PTSD as well as medical experts. Watching each episode, I couldn't help but think about my mother, who had lived her entire adult life struggling with manic depression, never really finding balance through prescription medication, hospitalization, or therapy. Could psychedelics have helped her and countless others like her?

Pollan, best known for his food writing (*The Omnivore's Dilemma* and *In Defense of Food*), perceives the study of psychedelics as a logical next step in exploring treatments for intractable conditions that affect the mind. We already tap into nature for everything from food to beauty supplies and homeopathics, so the concept of turning to naturally occurring substances to alter our consciousness fascinates Pollan, and I admit that I'm intrigued as well. My own natural consciousness raising includes a morning cup of tea to wake myself up, applying perfume to stimulate pheromones, and taking daily "forest baths" through Brooklyn's Prospect Park to feel more calm and centered. These are all examples of socially acceptable ways we access nature to alter our mindset. So why not include psychedelics as an effective and permissible route to higher consciousness as well? That said, I have never used psychedelics to alter my state of being, not because I am against them, but because they haven't been accessible to me, and I've never figured out a safe way to experience them.

There are certainly elements of life we cannot control, but we can control the anger, sadness, and fear that surround them. This is a journey of consciousness I, and many other people, explore in psychotherapy, but many others also find that a psychedelic trip can be the express lane on their highway to enlightenment. And the search for the perfect transformative substance continues in unlikely places, including the smoked venom of a Sonoran desert toad. Which begs the question, *Who was the first person who found a toad in a desert and thought that inhaling his venom was a good idea?*

* * *

I'm what most would consider to be a lightweight when it comes to alcohol. In high school, a cheap bottle of Annie Green Springs wine was passed around between me and my friends on the weekends, but I was never interested in getting drunk. Even as an adult, I've never craved alcohol, never much liked the taste, and never found it very fun to drink.

After my divorce, I stopped drinking entirely, for my teenage kids' sake. My ex's substance abuse had taken a toll on our family, and I wanted the kids to be able to trust that I would be physically and emotionally alert and available to them at all times. They are grown and launched now, but I am still a nondrinker. I haven't had an alcoholic beverage in over fifteen years. I do it for me. Not drinking alcohol is a triumphant celebration of my independence from decades of living with a substance abuser. For better or worse, I would rather eat my calories than drink them. I am not 'sober,' because I was never an alcoholic, and I don't presume to know the extraordinary struggle alcoholics in recovery face every day of their sobriety. I am a conscious nondrinker.

Do you trust yourself to know how much is enough when it comes to enjoying substances? If yes, has this always been the case?

Unfortunately, these days I find there are many social challenges being a single sixty-six-year-old nondrinker. On first dates, when prospective suitors find out I don't drink, they assume either that I am an alcoholic, or that I will automatically stand in judgment of their social lubricants. I'm so over it. I've had enough of being labeled for what I do or do not eat, smoke, or drink.

You Can't Change Anyone's Mind But Your Own

One of the most valuable and often challenging life lessons I've learned is that you cannot change anyone's mind but your own. This is a liberating realization. When you keep the focus on yourself and give others the dignity to make their own decisions, along with their own mistakes, everyone wins. Here are a few ways to incorporate this practice in your life:

1. Say "You know best." When friends, family, or coworkers are complaining out loud, fight the instinct to problem-solve. Simply say, "You know best," and mean it.
2. Wait to be asked for your opinion or advice. Often people just want to be heard, not fixed.
3. Set a daily goal to create small, intentional shifts to keep the focus on yourself. For example, you might set a timer on your phone to limit the length of calls from needy friends who zap your time and energy.

I remain vigilant about staying true to maintaining my own health and serenity. I am intimately aware of how charming, cunning, and charismatic alcoholics and drug addicts can be because the three great romantic loves of my life have all been in various stages of substance addiction or recovery. I pray that when I meet the fourth and hopefully final love of my life, I alone will be enough of a mind-bending intoxicant to satisfy all his cravings.

TAKE A DEEPER DIVE

*Has your life or the life of someone you love
been touched by substance abuse? What
have you learned from this experience?*

This is such a valuable exercise. Writing about your struggles with addiction, or those of a loved one, without anger or judgment can be the first step towards understanding and acceptance. The lessons learned are powerful because they usually boil down to finding the courage to create positive change in our lives.

*Is it the chronic substance use or the deception
and dishonesty that accompanies substance abuse
that would give you pause to say 'Enough'?*

This is a profound question to carefully contemplate. There are many layers of acknowledgement I had to go through before I decided to end my marriage. What moved you towards making a change in your life?

*What are the pros and cons of substance
use in your personal life?*

Create two columns and title one *Pros* and one *Cons*. List
ways you imbibe, people you imbibe with, and situations
that are more challenging with or without substances,
along with any other thoughts surrounding substances in
these Pro/Con columns. As you review the finished lists,
are you content with what you see?

CHAPTER 13

How Much Is Enough:

F U N

For me, fun is not optional. It is not frivolous or immature. It is as important as food, love, and deep, cleansing breaths. Fun is at the core of my healthiest relationships. Having fun is the most powerful seduction, in or out of bed. Fun has no age limit. If you are smart, you understand that you can never outgrow fun. One of the best compliments I ever received came from an astute five-year-old. After spending the afternoon with me, he asked his dad, "Is she a kid or a grown-up?"

I think of fun as an optic lens. When you look at life's everyday moments through this lens, you see new possibilities and the potential for fun in just about every setting. As I fall asleep each night and run through my day's activities, I often ask myself, "Did I have enough fun?" I wake up challenging myself to infuse fun in unexpected places. When I met my Brooklyn dentist for the first time, I greeted him by saying, "Greetings from your new favorite patient!" He cracked up, and we got off to a great start.

Everyone has a personal definition of fun. As a belief system, it is not dissimilar to spirituality. I can't tell you what is or isn't fun or funny. But I can tell you that fun, like spirituality, is a supreme coping skill, and I believe a daily dose will greatly improve the quality of your life.

* * *

I understood at a young age the social currency of being the fun one. As in most families, my siblings and I created our own distinct personal brands. My older brother loved music, my sister was the smart one, my little brother was the rabble-rouser, and I was the social one. Since we moved around a lot as children, I learned early that an upbeat personality attracted my kind of people. Fun begat fun. I wanted to hang out with the fun crowd. I sought that crowd in each new school I was enrolled in. I earned a reputation for having a good sense of humor early on, and I was proud of that. In middle school, I was crushed when I wasn't voted "Class Clown." I was sure I had all the right qualifications. My classmates thought otherwise. They voted me "Most Likely to Succeed." At fourteen years old, I had absolutely no idea what that meant.

* * *

At the end of my dad's life, he was deep in dementia. But that didn't prevent him from having fun. Telling the one joke he could remember—"Why are tomatoes red? Because they looked over the fence and saw Mrs. Green-pea"—to everyone who crossed his path was the highlight of his day. My dad's kooky sense of humor endured long after his memory had faded.

Is having enough fun part of your daily practice?

Science journalist Catherine Price believes in playfulness in everyday life. In her TED Talk, she calls fun a feeling rather than an activity. "Fun," she says, "is the secret to feeling alive. People that are having fun look like they are illuminated from within." I really love that visual.

Fun vs. Funny

My goal in exploring the concept of enough fun is not to turn everyone into comedians. Rather, I want to help draw your focus toward incorporating more joy into your life, even in darker days. Here are some suggestions for finding more fun in unexpected places.

1. Find fun through new accomplishments. Have fun by learning a new sport, mastering a new video game, or tracing your family tree. Fun does not always include laughter. It can be a challenging, focused activity that brings joy.
2. Incorporate new voices in your life. Discover authors like David Sedaris, artists like Ed Ruscha (visit his Chocolate Room!) and performers like Kate Berlant who will make you smile in unexpected ways.
3. Spend more time with children. To have fun, you have to be present, especially with kids. If you're not, you'll miss their brilliance. Children have a gift for seeking out fun in unexpected places. No one has more fun in an empty box than a child. They communicate through play and use fun as both a learning tool and a comprehensive tool. Why not join them?

Children speed-learn so many life lessons, from understanding the power of empathy to the subtleties of telling a successful fart joke. Stephanie Jones, a professor of early childhood development at Harvard University's Graduate School of Education, says, "In addition to promoting curiosity, exploration, and creativity, play provides children with the opportunity to practice important executive function and self-regulation skills like paying attention, inhibiting their impulses, and remembering and updating information." Yes, yes, all impressive, and in addition, very young children get full credit for originating the spit take.

* * *

As my own kids grew up, I was invested in being the fun mom in a fun house with a fun family. I set the stage the best I could, in and out of the house. Family vacations were often multigenerational and offered enough fun for everyone. We took several family cruises, and on one of them, my then preteen kids, who are three years apart in age, decided to embark for the week masquerading as fraternal twin siblings. My son was younger than but just as tall as his sister, so it wasn't hard to pull off. They shared their own stateroom along with their secret and had so much fun creating scenarios for their new identities. Who wouldn't enjoy having a twin for a week? Stories were creative and often nonsensical with the surprise benefit of creating an even deeper bond between them.

We loved to go to the movies as a family, and we often brought our kids' friends along. When I drove them to the local cineplex, I told them that they had to exchange pleasantries with the parking booth attendant with any accent of their choosing, foreign or imaginary. They were

What's the most fun you have had parenting?

equal parts embarrassed and enchanted by one of our greetings, which sounded something like, "Ello. Ears our moonie. Ank U airy mooch!"

Even after my kids grew up, I continued to invent new hijinks to inspire fun. One holiday weekend I had a house full of guests, including children who were not my own, I invited everyone out to the courtyard, where I had hidden dozens of Cool Whip–filled pie tins in the shrubbery. When asked why everyone was invited outside, I pulled a pie out of a bush and yelled, "PIE FIGHT!" at the top of my lungs. The next few moments were a blur of running, squealing, Cool Whip–covered guests, utterly surprised and delighted over this spontaneous outburst of messy fun. I'll never forget it, and neither will my guests.

* * *

One of the new friends I've made since moving to Brooklyn is my neighbor Scott Ginsberg, who personifies fun in his work and his life. When Scott was a junior in college, he attended an event that required everyone to wear a name tag. After the event was over, he decided to leave his name tag on. He was shocked to see how easy it suddenly became to make new friends, meet girls, and attract flurries of attention. He turned this accidental social experiment into his profession and personal brand, even becoming the *Ripley's Believe It or Not* world record holder for name tag wearing. No one embraces a personal brand quite like Scott. He even had his original, "Hi my name is Scott" name tag tattooed on his chest.

Scott considers himself an ideal case study on human interaction, revolutionizing the way people look at approachability, identity, and commitment. Scott knows how to enter a room, command the right kind of attention, and bring just enough fun and self-confidence to make sure no one forgets his name.

* * *

After retiring as a stand-up, I toured the US as a humor consultant. My company, FunnyWorks, was hired by a wide range of businesses to improve hiring practices, prevent burnout, and improve company morale. One luxury hotel general manager hired me, admitting, "We know how to find skilled staff, but we also want to hire staff who understand, embrace, and communicate fun." Professionals including physicians at Kaiser Permanente, San Francisco real estate developers, Nevada coal miners, American Agri-women, and matrimonial attorneys were energized and encouraged to have more fun at work through my interactive keynotes and workshops.

Are you having enough fun at work? If the answer is no, what's holding you back?

It took me years to research, collect the stories, and conduct the interviews for my book, *Funny Works! 52 Ways to Have More Fun at Work, Plus 52 Ways to Have Even More Fun at Home.* I followed every lead I had to understand the power of humor and uncover success stories of professionals who embraced the power of fun in the workplace. It convinced me that fun plays an essential role in personal and professional longevity and success.

Accountants rarely get credit for their sense of humor, but my brother told me a workplace story that should be compelling enough to change your mind. When he worked as an auditor at KPMG, they audited a chocolate manufacturer. One part of the audit involved calculating the quantity of chocolate in the various vats on the production floor. My brother explained, "The timing of the audit was such that our audit team always included one brand-new accountant right out of college. Every year, the rest of the team, along with the chocolate company employees, would rent a scuba diving suit and tell the new accountant that they needed to don the suit and dive into the tank to make sure there wasn't a false bottom that would misstate the quantity of chocolate. The new person, not wanting to question authority, would put on the wetsuit and walk out into the warehouse where there would be dozens of people snapping photos as the newbie came through the door. Once they were let off the hook, they had the final laugh and always took the prank in stride."

Pranks like these are harmless and provide memorable, fun stories told long after the prank is over. One of the most famous Hollywood pranksters is George Clooney, legendary for planning elaborate pranks on his costars. One of his most famous involved coconspirators, the studio wardrobe tailors. They implemented George's top-secret prank to take in costar Matt Damon's pants just a sliver of an inch every day, giving Matt pause to worry that he was gaining weight. This went on for weeks until Matt finally got wise to the prank.

* * *

There's been fascinating research done on the medical benefits of laughter. Psychoneuroimmunology studies have shown that laughter can have a positive effect on your mental and physical health and even your ability to manage pain. This medical research shows that laughter and a positive mental attitude can temporarily increase the release of immunoglobulin A, boosting your immune system and influencing antiviral immunity such as your Covid vaccine response. Laughter has even been proven to lower blood pressure and release tension in our bodies. I know a couple's counselor who had a creative way to help clients defuse marital

How has incorporating fun into your life impacted your health?

tension. She gave them a key phrase to use when tempers flared. The rule was when one or the other said this phrase, the couple had to stop arguing and move to separate rooms. The assigned phrase was, "I have to go to the bathroom." It not only calmed tempers, it often lightened the mood enough to shift the energy. Inevitably, someone would start giggling, triggering the end of the argument. It's a moving example of powerful mind–body connection and the undeniable power of fun.

Dr. Edward Dunkelblau is a licensed clinical psychologist and nationally acclaimed expert on the topics of social-emotional intelligence, humor, and health. He reports, "If we were talking about a prescription that had all the physiological effects, all the psychological effects, and the potential immunological effects of laughter, the FDA would be on it like crazy, regulating it and running trials." Add a dose of Viagra, and I predict our nation's divorce rate would drop by at least 50 percent.

* * *

When I was an improv actor at The Second City in Chicago, one of the first rules I learned was, "Yes, and . . . ." We learned that the minute we said *no* on stage or denied the reality another improv actor had created, we had basically wrecked the scene. By saying yes, fun, fantastical stories could be created on stage between castmates based on audience suggestions. I chose to adopt this philosophy in other aspects of my life, and I am still enjoying the benefits of "Yes, and . . ." to this day. Making the conscious choice to say yes, even when I feel hesitant or afraid, creates fun new career opportunities and social adventures. I become emboldened to take more chances and find more fun through this simple approach.

> Can you cite an example from your own life where an injection of humor was enough to improve a prickly situation?

And just in case you were wondering, yes, this extends to my dating life. At sixty-six years old, I have no patience for humorless suitors. If I'm not having enough fun on a date, often there is a swift reckoning, followed by a polite exit. Middle-life dating must be fun, or really, what's the point? And let me tell you, times have really changed. When I was a decade younger, my dates would try and impress me with their fancy cars. Now they love flashing their handicap vehicle placards. Having a sense of humor is the quickest way to my heart, my bedroom, and a prime parking space.

My family, and I hope yours, take fun very seriously. It is a form of communication currency. Our commitment to having fun has softened the blows of divorce, addiction, illness, and the loss of loved ones. My son now wears the cap that defines our family's life philosophy. We bought the same cap for my dad at Disneyland decades ago. He wore it throughout his eighties and into his nineties, through his years in dementia. It's the one that is embroidered with the words "I'm never growing up" in a child's scrawl.

TAKE A DEEPER DIVE

What role does fun play in your daily life?

Here's a great way to find out: For one whole day, use a journal or the notepad app on your phone to do a conscious inventory of where you find fun. Record every time you find yourself smiling and feeling that boost that only fun can offer. Some examples of where I find fun in my day include looking at life through my granddaughters' eyes, eavesdropping on other people's phone calls in public places, making fun of my groceries with the supermarket checkout clerk, and joking about my two left feet in Zumba class.

Do you think one can have too much fun?

As a humor consultant for businesses, I was often surprised and disappointed when employees confided that they were afraid to have fun at work because they thought they might appear unprofessional. I'm sure you can think of other places and occasions where having too much fun would be frowned upon. What, in your opinion, is an example of *too much fun?*

***Do you believe a sense of fun is a conscious
choice or an innate instinct?***

Make a list of people you know who are naturally funny.
Now list people you know who make a conscious effort to
"find the funny." Would you put yourself on either of these
lists? If not, explore why. Next, think about your friends.
Whom do you consider your go-to friend when you want
to have fun? List the qualities you admire most about this
friend and how they bring fun into your life.

CHAPTER 14

How Much Is Enough:

EDUCATION

Are you educated enough about all the things you really care about in life? An education is not just an acquisition. Nor is it a destination. I am a student of my own life, so, for me, class is always in session. How much is enough education depends upon everything from socioeconomics to nagging parents, combined with your own innate curiosity about the world. I believe we are all born with a unique set of gifts to cultivate and develop through an education, but often our deepest growth and awakening to our own talents and abilities take place outside a traditional classroom. An education is not just about grades or seeking the approval of a teacher. For me, an education is an ignition switch that, when turned on, taps into my passion and purpose and gives me validation, direction, and a hunger for more knowledge.

My mother was my all-time favorite educator. She was one of four children, the only daughter. Her mother, an ambitious businesswoman, owned a high-end Chicago retail clothing store and had little interest in motherhood or raising her four children. She paid scant attention to my mom and saw no point in investing time or money in her dreams or her education.

Who taught you the most profound lessons in your life?

My mom was a child on a desperate search for love. She rarely received a sideways glance from her mother, so she gravitated toward her Aunt Emma, my grandmother's sister, who was witty, extravagantly stylish, and unconditionally loving and supportive. Aunt Emma was an important, supportive role model who encouraged my mom's dreams of becoming a teacher.

When my mom was accepted into the University of Illinois, her parents refused to pay her tuition. They considered educating a woman a waste of money and chose to finance their sons' college tuitions instead. Emma gave my mother enough money to go to college, and my mother was committed to making the most of her aunt's generosity and showing her parents what a mistake they made by writing her off as "only a woman."

Once my mother settled into her 1940s college coed life, she came to realize that she'd had enough of being treated as "less than" because she was a woman. Her sense of justice deepened as she found a community of like-minded students at the University of Illinois who organized civil rights protests around the campus. They had experienced enough racism, antisemitism, and misogyny to know that the world needed to change. Students of all colors, nationalities, religions, and backgrounds stood together and successfully closed a local restaurant that refused to serve Black patrons.

Did you find enough value in your education when you were young?

My mom proudly left college with a bachelor's degree and also a thick FBI file that documented her civil rights activism. She graduated with a deep conviction to stand for what she believed was right and fair for all. Hers was a multifaceted education that influenced the rest of her life and touched mine in a profound way.

Both my parents were proud of their educations. My dad earned his engineering degree while working full time and fathering young children—no easy task. Parenthood shifted their financial priorities. My mom stopped teaching to become a stay-at-home parent, and my father became the sole, stressed-out breadwinner. My parents were solid middle class with no disposable income. There wasn't money for all the things we begged for because, unbeknownst to us, they were making sure there was enough money saved to send all four of us to college. As a child who fancied herself a budding movie star, I moaned about not having enough new clothes, cosmetics, and trendy tchotchkes. But as an adult, I was deeply appreciative to begin my post-graduation life without the burden of college debt.

* * *

In high school, I was a lackadaisical student. We had just moved from Southern California to a Chicago suburb, and I was harboring a huge grudge toward my parents for moving us back to the Midwest. Everyone in my new high school had basically grown up together, so cliques were tight and ran deep. I was also the first Jewish student most of my new classmates had met, and the antisemitism was subtle but palpable. When a high school football player told me he was surprised I didn't have horns growing out of my head, as his father told him all Jews did, I realized I was a long way from my old California community where being Jewish was as commonplace as the palm trees that lined the neighborhood streets.

Was a formal education a financial priority in your family? Was there enough money to go to college?

Once I, the displaced and disgruntled California girl, started getting cast in plays in my Midwest high school, I felt a sense of accomplishment and belonging. I finally had enough of a reason to want to go to high school. My grades remained unremarkable, and I got the third lowest grade on my college entrance exams. My college counselor, Miss Gurbacki, told my parents it would be a waste of money to send me off to college, but my mother, still stinging from her own parents' having written her off, refused to do that to me. She admonished Miss Gurbacki for not taking enough time to get to know me, and she made sure I knew that she and my dad were 100 percent behind my college dreams.

I graduated high school at sixteen, got early acceptance to Illinois State University, and excitedly headed right to college. I had ignorantly assumed that all parents pay for their children's education. Then I met Lori, a short, scrappy twenty-seven-year-old fellow freshman in my dorm who immediately revealed herself to be far more mature than me in many fundamental ways. She wanted to save enough money so she wouldn't have to take out loans. Her wardrobe was sparse and basic, and her frugality made me reevaluate my own personal style and spending habits. Meeting her gave me a deeper appreciation for the lifetime of sacrifices my parents had made to afford my siblings' and my college educations.

I dove headfirst into college life. With reckless exuberance, I joined every club, auditioned for every play, and attended every party advertised with a flier posted on our dorm's bulletin board. Moving out of my family home and into my college dorm was exhilarating. I felt like I had been shot nude out of a confetti cannon. Not having enough common sense to pace myself, I ended up with a whopping case of mononucleosis that sent me to the hospital and then home for three weeks during my first semester. When I returned to college, I was urged by the dean of students to withdraw and redo the semester. I refused. I saw this as a personal challenge and a way to show my parents I was not going to waste their money. I buckled down, stopped gazing out my dorm window at all the coed streakers, and started spending more time in the library than at frat-house keggers. And what do you know? I made the dean's list by the end of my first tumultuous semester of college.

Was there someone in your life who gave you a deeper appreciation for your education?

At Illinois State University in Normal, Illinois, I made a point to cram as much practical life training in between my classroom studies as possible. As I alluded to in the Work chapter, I designed my own college education, crafting a "contract" major that would cross multiple departments, including theater, journalism, and radio and television broadcasting. Attending classes wasn't enough to convince my advisor that this was a viable major. So I performed in plays, worked as the late-night DJ at the college radio station, and became the weather and news reporter for the college TV station. I also wrote for the college newspaper, crafting a weekly arts column and reviewing all the theater productions I hadn't gotten cast in. This was all in an effort to show my advisor that my degree had practical value in my life.

Of course, like many coeds in the 1970s, I enjoyed more than enough smoke-filled rock concerts, on- and off-campus parties, sexual escapades, and an array of other questionable behaviors. During visits home, I would often tell my parents that my college education had more to do with extracurriculars than textbooks. They could see that I was thriving. I really loved college and the person I became there. Unlike my haphazard high school years, I now flourished as an organized, conscientious student, shocking my parents with solid GPAs every semester. I swear it wasn't to spite my counselor, Miss Gurbacki, for having written me off as an academic loser in high school, but a part of me delighted in proving her so miserably wrong.

When did you know you'd had enough formal education?

I was excited to graduate college and begin my post-college life, but many of my friends went on to get advanced degrees in law, business, or other fields. Some couldn't find a job, and getting another degree became an expensive stall tactic. Medical school seemed to me like an interminable amount of education, and to this day, I remain in complete awe of the singular focus required to become a medical professional. Not to mention the high tolerance for blood.

* * *

As a very young child, I was anxious to get out of the house and begin my education. I finished high school by my sixteenth year and couldn't wait to graduate college a semester early at the tender age of twenty.

These days, I wonder why I was in such a rush to put formal education behind me because I remain passionately committed to being a student for life. Since I've been out of school, I've learned valuable lessons in an array of unexpected locales. My favorite nontraditional classrooms have been comedy clubs, television sound stages, and, of course, my family home. I've gained a deeper sense of self in my therapist's office, through travel, and in Al-Anon meetings. The lessons that have had the most profound and enduring impact on my priorities are those gleaned from caring for my aging parents, my children, and, now, my grandchildren, who remind me how pure, unfiltered, sticky, and LOUD true love can be.

Continuing Education

Continuing your education has less to do with a classroom and more to do with staying curious about the world. Follow your passions and remain a student with the following inspiration:

1. Explore existing passions from a different angle. Enjoy riding your bike? Book a trip through Backroads.com

to travel the world with those who share your love for cycling. Do you enjoy sewing and needlework? Attend local textile conventions to reinvigorate your passion and connect with others. Are you a fan of fly fishing? Discover a new territory in which to pull up your waders and cast your line.

2. Stay current with technology. Don't be intimidated by new gadgets. Be aware and surround yourself with people who know more than you and are willing to teach you enough to bolster your confidence. The resulting multigenerational exchange of information and ideas will add richness to your life.

3. Learn more about your community, your state, and your country. Take walking tours of your town, join a current events discussion group, and plan a tour of your state or nation's capital. Narrow the divide with civic pride.

My most impactful teachers have been my children. Throughout their lives, I've had to check myself to make sure I was the parent they needed and deserved. As a stand-up comedian, I crafted my material thoughtfully, constantly asking myself if my children would be embarrassed to hear what was coming out of my mouth. When I was contemplating my eventual divorce, I thought hard about the impact it would have on my kids. I am keenly aware that they have been paying close attention throughout our lives together. Now that they are grown and lead independent lives, the lessons have shifted, but we continue to be each other's teachers.

* * *

My two children had very different educational experiences, which shouldn't come as a surprise, since they are such different kinds of people.

My daughter, Jenna, was always a serious student, the kind of kid who needs reminders to stop studying, relax, and have fun. From sixth grade through twelfth, she went to an all-girls school—the environment where girls learn best, according to compelling data.

> **Do you think our current public education system gives enough credence to the different ways boys and girls learn?**

Dr. Diana Meehan Goldberg, one of the founders of my daughter's alma mater, The Archer School for Girls, understood that girls process and learn differently from boys. At a prospective family welcome night, she proved her point with a traditional math story problem: "If a train leaves the Los Angeles train station on a Monday, going 100 mph, how long will it take to get to New York, 2,781 miles away? The male student will immediately raise his hand, still calculating in his head but confident that he will arrive at an answer by the time the teacher calls on him, which most often happens just to move the lesson along. The female student will need more time, most likely processing a wide array of information before arriving at the exact same answer as her male counterpart: How many train cars are there? Are there sleeper cars? Is there a dining car? What are they serving? Are there children on the train? Do they have coloring books?"

I have no doubt that my daughter grew up to be the bright, confident, compassionate person that she is today due in no small part to same-sex education during her formative years. I know firsthand how distracting a coed education can be. I have no doubt that the countless hours I spent in middle school and high school oohing and obsessing about my male classmates could have been better spent in pursuit of academic excellence.

* * *

I knew my son was a musician from the time he started banging a beat on his high chair tray with his Mickey Mouse spoon. He had little interest in formal education and constantly questioned its relevance to his daily life. He was often misunderstood and misdiagnosed by teachers and school counselors, many of whom wrote him off as a distractible miscreant. I was warned that he had learning differences that included reading comprehension challenges. I would listen patiently, nod, and think to myself, *This is the same twelve-year-old who had enough moxie and comprehension skills to save enough money to buy a sound mixer, digested the 150-page manual over a weekend, and understood enough of it to start producing his own recordings of his compositions.* Reading comprehension wasn't my son's problem. His lack of connection to the subject matter was the problem.

Both of my kids went to college. My daughter graduated from Brandeis University, then earned her master's from the London School of Economics. But my son made a compelling case for dropping out. After his freshman year, he was offered a summer internship that became an impressive job offer and a tantalizing launch pad into the music industry. This was his dream job, one he would have been grateful to nab upon graduation. But here it was now, and he felt ready to leap. He told his dad and me that the music industry valued youth, and if he started his career at nineteen, he'd have several years of professional experience under his belt by the time his competitors graduated college. He promised to re-enroll for college courses when and if he felt the need, and we trusted him enough to support his decision. And his prescient plan turned out to be 100 percent correct.

* * *

Many students today are questioning the value of a college degree and weighing their earning potential in their chosen field against the crushing loans that quickly mount. Does it make sense for an Early Childhood major to incur over $100,000 of debt to earn an average annual salary of $43,236?

In what ways do you feel formal education has been instrumental in your personal or professional success?

For many creative endeavors, practical work experience can be of greater value than a college degree. Students interested in a culinary career may choose to obtain a degree at the Culinary Institute of America, where tuition and fees are over $50,000 a year. But most successful professional chefs will tell you that time spent honing your skills in a culinary internship at your best neighborhood restaurant will be enough to help you gain the same acumen and be assured of full-time employment.

* * *

The term *special education* always confused me. The stereotypes of my childhood perpetuated the myth that kids with learning differences are less intelligent than the "normal" kids and unable to excel in school. But I have come to believe that everyone lives on some kind of educational spectrum, with some degree of a learning difference. Many of

Did anyone ever tell you that you weren't "college material"? Did you believe them?

us have an array of reading challenges; others struggle with attention deficits, comprehension, processing speed, or retention. Students with social challenges associated with autism may not make great eye contact, but they can often retain volumes of information and focus like a laser on subjects they love.

Today, more and more college students take Adderall whether or not a doctor prescribes it because they feel it sharpens their focus. This seems ironic to me considering how many of these same students are also smoking pot, which offers pretty much the opposite effect.

Why don't more people believe they have enough competency to succeed in school without feeling insecure about their GPA? And really, in most of our chosen professions, who cares about our GPA? I have never, in my fifty years of employment, been asked by a boss, an HR director, or a comedy club owner for my GPA. Why aren't other qualifications, like real, honest-to-God life experiences, enough to tip the scales in a job applicant's favor?

Do you think you learned enough practical life skills at school?

Covid Zoom school was a haven for autodidacts. Left to their own unique ability, rhythm, and passion for learning, these self-motivated students set their own pace and often their own curriculum. While in high school, I often fantasized about learning independently outside the classroom, but knew I was too easily distracted, and I had to acknowledge that I didn't have enough discipline and maturity to teach myself. To be completely honest, just thinking about what I'd be having for lunch would be distracting enough to pull me out of my morning studies. Especially if potato chips were on the menu.

For younger students, Covid Zoom school was a huge setback. The Brookings Institution released a research study in January 2022 that tracked math and reading scores across the first two years of the pandemic. They compared test scores from immediately before the pandemic in the fall of 2019, a year later in the fall of 2020, and then again in the fall of 2021 and 2022. There was a sizable drop in test scores for kids in grades three through eight. Teachers made their best effort to meet the challenge, scrambling for ways to reach through the screen to connect students with their virtual studies. But it wasn't enough. This age group also had a marked increase in depression, self-harm, and suicide. They missed their friends, the spontaneous hallway meet-and-greets, locker chats, lunchtime, school dances, after-school clubs, sporting events, and furtive parking lot make out sessions, all essential facets of an adolescent's school life.

Test scores are a way to measure academic progress, but they rarely tell the complete story of a student's unique gifts. I was never a fan of standardized testing because I believe that the scores are too specific and not enough of a reflection of each student's myriad talents and abilities. And yes, I formed this opinion based on my own abysmal standardized test scores. When it came time for my kids to take their college entrance exams, I bristled at the concept of test prep coaching, believing it was just a way for affluent families to game the system. What is the point of tricking a school into thinking my kids are a certain sort of student because they tested well? I assured my kids that they would be accepted to the right college for them, regardless of whether or not they took an expensive test prep course. My idea of appropriate preparation for entrance exams was simply arriving with freshly sharpened pencils.

I am a forever student. Reflecting back, I compare my continuing education to one of those massive tool boxes with multiple unfolding tiers of trays, slots, and compartments. You always have enough room to cram one more tool or gadget into one of these boxes. And thanks to my ever-changing technology—*oy vey, Apple! How many updates do we really need?*—I always have something new to learn. Age is never an excuse to stop learning. My brain may not be young, but my wit is quick, my hunger insatiable, and my sense of wonder, boundless.

TAKE A DEEPER DIVE

Who was your all-time favorite teacher?

Write a fan letter to the teacher who had the greatest, most enduring impact on your life. You need not mail this letter, though you can if you want to. As you write your fan letter, consider these questions: What was it about this teacher that made them so impactful? Was it their character? Their teaching style? Their personality? How did this teacher give you enough confidence to become your best self in their class? How have their lessons stayed with you through adulthood?

Knowing what you know now, what advice would you give your younger self about choosing an academic path?

Reflect on how your education impacted who you are today. Take that knowledge and write a letter to your younger self, filled with loving advice and guidance.

Do you believe you have both an EQ—emotional intelligence—and an IQ—intellectual intelligence?

Daniel Goleman's book *Emotional Intelligence,* published in 1995, became an international best seller and established a new framework for thinking about soft skills. Goleman writes, "Emotional intelligence can help people make better decisions. It defines our capacity for relationship." Goleman's theory is that people who possess these characteristics have a far greater chance of being successful than those who do not. Share some examples of how both EQ and IQ play a role in your personal and professional life.

CHAPTER 15

How Much Is Enough:

B E A U T Y

Venice, Italy, is arguably one of the most beautiful cities in the world, an archipelago of magnificently constructed hamlets and waterways, where newlyweds travel for the ultimate honeymoon. In Venice, no one goes hungry. A sublime serving of pasta can be had in any of the centuries-old trattorias found in every curvy alleyway, all beautiful enough to photograph and post on your Instagram page. Venice attracts visitors from around the world who marvel at the splendor, pray in the churches, and dance in the Piazza Saint Marco. But it was the tourists who rode the gondolas who caught my eye and inspired me to write this chapter, in which I reflect on where we find and define beauty and how we choose to capture it.

Every day I spent in Venice, I spotted tourists in gondolas armed with selfie sticks, shooting close-ups of themselves as the gondoliers carefully navigated their iconic hand-painted boats through the narrow canals. Ornate stained-glass windows shot colorful rays of light into the canals; decorative moldings adorned each building like icing on a wedding cake. Intricate brickwork and hand-carved sculptures were everywhere. None of this beauty was captured in the tourists' selfies. No architectural details. Not even a sliver of the wary, costumed gondoliers, whom I often caught rolling their eyes with exhausted exasperation to no one in particular, muttering under their breath what I could only guess was Italian for, *"For this I dropped out of med school?"*

Over and over I watched and wondered at what point these people would have enough pictures of themselves to put the camera down, look around, be in the moment, and just take in the beauty of the locale. Why did they care more about photographing themselves than experiencing the beauty surrounding them?

This selfie scenario is played out everywhere from vacations to children's birthday parties. Years from now, when we look at these photos, will we even remember where or why they were taken? And really, who are these selfies for? Is the beauty we believe we are capturing in these shots enough to catch the eye of a stranger who will change the course of our future? Will our gaze be riveting enough to make an ex think twice about breaking up with us? Are we capturing our beauty in a futile ploy to stop time, keeping us ageless, if not forever, then just for this moment? Was Dorian Gray the originator of the selfie?

What's the most beautiful place you've ever visited?

Picture Perfect

Go on a deep dig through all your photos to find pictures you feel best define each decade of your life. Print and paste these photos into a lined journal so you can write about what you see when you look at each photo from your present-day perspective. Here are some writing prompts to help you reflect on each photo:

1. What made me feel most beautiful at this age?
2. Who were my biggest supporters who gave me enough confidence to feel beautiful?

3. Knowing what I know now, what would I tell myself at each age and stage of life that would have provided the impetus to move forward with positivity?
4. Write yourself a heartfelt compliment for each decade.

How many of us make a conscious effort to look for the beauty around us on a daily basis? Where do you see beauty: In nature? In architecture? In a perfect half-court free throw? In a fresh-baked, symmetrically latticed pie?

* * *

During my teens, I began to understand the concept of physical beauty as social validation. As I've aged, the word *beautiful* has gradually been replaced with *presentable* as I gaze into my morning mirror. Flouncy dresses have been replaced most days with stretchy yoga pants that have yet to be worn inside of a yoga studio.

On the streets of New York, one of the most fashion-conscious cities in the world, I am acutely aware of all the beauty that surrounds me. I am at ease in the knowledge that, at this stage of my life, I am more or less transparent, if not invisible. I say this not to elicit pity but rather to reveal a superpower. I actually like and appreciate my sixty-something invisibility. It fills me with a deeper sense of my own beauty. I have knowledge, perspective, and self-awareness I did not possess in my twenties that I am grateful to have today. I can feel beautiful and feel seen even when no one is looking. My face, my body, and my overall health are beautiful enough, strong enough, and 100 percent my own. My beauty is not defined by social media, a dress size, an eyelash extension, a romantic partner, or a second glance from a perfect stranger.

I am relieved to admit that I am no longer interested in comparing my beauty to anyone else's.

* * *

As a young college theater major unable to get cast as an ingenue in anything, I reluctantly accepted my status as a character actor. I was comforted by the knowledge that I would never age out of my look, only grow deeper into it. I knew by the time I was eighteen that I would never be categorized as traditionally beautiful, either in theatrical productions or in life. Men would not be mesmerized by my beauty. My looks would not stop traffic, nor would I ever be able to use it as currency. On the plus side, I was taken seriously, listened to, and treated with a different sort of respect that came more from what I knew than how I looked, and all that was very helpful as I launched my career in comedy.

At what point in your life did you come to understand your own unique brand of beauty?

Women in comedy, especially in the 1980s when I was performing in clubs, were not expected to be beautiful. How we looked did not matter as much as how funny we were. It was enough that we were able to command attention with our words, our wit, our timing, and our comebacks. As a young comedian, I believed I was sufficiently fetching to attract attention, but not so much as to distract audiences from my material. I sought a different kind of approval from my audiences.

* * *

So, how beautiful is beautiful enough? What's the delicate line that separates the classic beauties from the handsome, the pleasant, the stylish, the interesting, the unusual, the quirky, and every other brand of nontraditional beauty? And at what age do we—whether we are male, female, trans or nonbinary—cast ourselves as classically or nontraditionally beautiful?

As a very young child, I knew I could always get a strong, immediately positive response by posing for pictures with my head tilted, my clasped hands against one cheek, and an impish grin. I can't remember if I felt beautiful doing it, but I knew that goofy pose made grown-ups smile and that was enough for me.

As a child, did you ever feel "less than" because you didn't look a certain way? How did you counteract that feeling?

I will admit this much: when I am showered, shampooed, dressed, and made up, I do feel more beautiful. During the pandemic, when I came in contact with no one, it was easy to shimmy down the apathy rabbit hole, staying in sweats and often skipping my morning shower. Bravo if you cut your own hair during the pandemic. You were much braver than me. I just let it grow. These days, simply wearing something with a fitted waistband is enough to change my aura and enhance my self-confidence. What makes me feel beautiful is simply putting my best foot forward, even if that foot is wearing a furry house slipper.

Because I firmly believe real beauty presents itself at every age, I've never been a fan of those fashion guides that dictate how we should dress during each decade of life. I believe you are as beautiful as you feel, and more power to you if that means wearing a strappy mini-dress and stiletto heels at eighty. I often find myself walking behind someone who is dressed super trendy and fully accessorized. I stroll ahead, look back into their face, and see a person in their seventies. I smile at this member of my aspirational tribe, a kindred spirit who refuses to fall into the stereotype of "dressing for our age."

* * *

My son lives in West Hollywood, California, half a block from Melrose Boulevard, where one ultra-stylish boutique after another attempts to display, define, and sell beauty. The Paul Smith clothing store at the end of his block features a giant pink exterior wall where people from around the world flock to take selfies. Out my son's balcony window, I watch a seemingly endless parade of people arch their backs and tilt their faces toward this wall under the bizarre impression that this color holds some mystical power to make them look beautiful. They'll even hoist babies against this wall for their birth announcements—as if babies need any augmented reality to be beautiful.

What role does social media play in your definition of beauty?

I thought that wall was an isolated locus of insanity until I visited the island of Burano, Italy where each row house is painted in bright, beautiful colors. I laughed out loud when I saw a throng of posers in front of a residence that was painted Barbie-pink. Clearly I am woefully ignorant of the powers of this magical color.

* * *

And speaking of color, gray is my new favorite color. Three years ago, I decided to stop coloring my hair, an expensive and futile charade I had been perpetuating for decades. My decision was met with skepticism from both friends and family who feared it would prematurely age me. I laughed this off and felt incredibly liberated with my decision. My hair is now a dozen gloriously gradient shades of gray, longer, thicker, and healthier than it has ever been. My gray hair is beautiful and unique enough to get compliments from complete strangers, many of which are women who confess they are too self-conscious to let their own hair go gray.

In America, beauty is too often linked to our appearance. More specifically, our body weight. Can a larger person be valued for their beauty? Absolutely, and even more so in other countries. In Italy, I am always impressed when I see women of all ages and sizes in bikinis at the community pools and beaches. Utterly unselfconscious, they are comfortable in their own skin, and no one in Italian society appears to outwardly question otherwise.

In Benin, West Africa, men point with pride at their large wives. It shows the family is prosperous. A well-fed wife is a sign of a successful, passionate life. Around the world, tattoos often illustrate a personal expression of beauty. In the Māori culture, the moko tradition involves tattooing your chin to attract a partner. Each moko is unique and depicts specific ancestral information.

Throughout India, kohl eyeliner, facial piercings, and ornate henna designs are traditional touches of beauty when prepping for fancy occasions. I've always harbored a secret wish to be a Bollywood star just to be able to wear all those gorgeous adornments.

In America, people spend thousands on spray tans to replicate a beautiful, sun-kissed glow. But in many Asian cultures, pale skin signifies wealth. Tan skin is equated with laborers who work outdoors, constantly exposed to the sun. In Korea, pale skin is the ultimate expression of beauty. So much so that women will spend exorbitant amounts of money to bleach their skin.

In indigenous tribes of South America and for the Mursi or Suri in Ethiopia, a lip dilator signifies that a girl has become a woman. As a thirteen-year-old American Jewish girl, all I had to do to make my passage into womanhood was learn Hebrew and read from the Torah at my Bat Mitzvah.

And to think I foolishly complained about that. Here's what these Ethiopian teens must endure: To signify their womanhood, young tribal females remove their two lower front teeth, engrave their lip, and insert a clay or wood disc to make their lip widen. Every year, a bigger disk is added so the older they are, the more beautiful they appear in their culture. Parents of teenagers, feel free to mention this the next time your teens whine about their orthodonture.

What sort of pain or discomfort are you willing to endure in the name of beauty?

In the Masai tribe, elongated earlobes are the ultimate expression of beauty. The status of a woman is evaluated by her lobe's length, size, and amount of jewelry adorning each ear.

I always admired Audrey Hepburn's long, graceful neck, but I would never go to the extremes that many women in Myanmar and Thailand go to achieve an elongated neck. As children, females wear a brass ring around their neck, and every year, a family member will add one or two more rings until they are adults. They believe that the longer your neck appears, the more beautiful you are. Adult women can wear up to fifty-five rings, totaling more than twenty-four pounds of jewelry around their necks. After reading this, I'm going to think twice before I complain about wearing an itchy turtleneck sweater.

As exotic and painful as many of these definitions of beauty sound, I have to wonder what other cultures think of the way American women, and increasingly men, resort to plastic surgery to achieve a certain perceived standard of beauty.

And how young should a parent sanction plastic surgery for their teens? The FDA has not approved injectable lip fillers for anyone under twenty-one, but tell that to the way too many kissy-faced teens of Beverly Hills. If plastic surgery is your chosen road toward beauty, at what point do you finally pull off that road and say, 'Enough is enough'? Is there a moment where a person who has spent their self-deprecating life nipping, tucking, pulling, starving, microplaning, and injecting, finally accepts their beauty? I sincerely pray for that profound, self-loving, revelatory moment for all of us.

TAKE A DEEPER DIVE

Do you have a go-to outfit that makes you feel especially beautiful?

Describe in detail the clothes, shoes, jewelry, undergarments, even the perfume that make you smile with satisfaction when you look in the mirror. How often do you wear this ensemble? To what events? What is it about this outfit that makes you feel so special? Is it the color, fit, or texture or price tag? Is this outfit connected to a happy memory? Did you buy it for yourself or was it a gift?

Besides physical appearance, what represents beauty in your life?

Let your imagination go wild and make an unedited list of the first things that comes to mind—anything from an opera, a fragrant blooming rose, or an infant's smile. There are absolutely no wrong answers here, and this list will give you and anyone you care to share it with a deeper glimpse into your heart.

Who represents your ideal definition of beauty and why?

As you contemplate this question, please don't limit yourself to only physical beauty. Take a moment to think about what makes someone beautiful inside and out. List at least five people, along with a brief explanation of why they made your list. What qualities do they possess that you would like to emulate?

CHAPTER 16

How Much Is Enough:

M E M O R Y

Memories are all we have to tell our story. Many people may embellish or outright lie about theirs, but memories are the chain-links to our history. I have a small pile of photos and a few home movies that document my childhood, along with my memories. My siblings can confirm (or deny) momentous family experiences like vacations or holidays, but many of my day-to-day childhood memories are uniquely mine, and so, with my parents both gone, I am the sole keeper of these ephemeral recollections. Are these memories enough to create a complete map of my life?

My earliest childhood memory is convincing my parents and our school principal that at four years old, I could read an entire book and was mature enough to enter kindergarten. I wanted to go to school so desperately that I had my mom read me the same storybook every night for weeks, memorizing the words along with when she would turn each page. I brought this book with me to my kindergarten interview where I met the principal, a gray-haired man with a kind smile. We sat in his dark, wood-paneled office, and after a few simple color recognition exercises and some impressive block stacking, I proceeded to 'read' him my book. My strong memory and audacious initiative was enough to get me accepted a year

What is your earliest memory?

early into kindergarten. Flash forward sixty-two years. The title of that life-changing book? I have no clue.

There is still much to learn about our unique neuroscience and how our brains process and store information. As I've gotten older, I am acutely aware of how quickly I can lose a train of thought and how random and bizarre my memory bank seems to be. Sometimes I imagine my brain like an old-fashioned Rolodex, endlessly spinning with cards filled with scrawled information in janky handwriting. I am mystified when I struggle to remember a beloved family member's name while being able to immediately access several sitcom theme songs from the 1970s. Why is my brain storing obscure pop culture facts and trivia ahead of the important stuff? And is this the foretelling of my own mental decline? And where are my keys?

When I care for my granddaughters, my memories flash fast and bright, like a summer lightning storm. They take me back to precious memories of raising my own children, attempting to capture moments that did not include any momentous occasion, just a little gushy, spontaneous, outpouring of love. I vividly remember holding my toddlers' hands, feeling their trusting squeeze, and looking down to see their eyes gazing up at me with such sweetness. I remember thinking, *Claire, remember this moment. Put this in your memory bank for when they grow up and away from you.*

Make Your Own Memories

- What do you want people to remember about you? There are many ways to preserve your memory. Here are a few of my favorites:
- Print favorite family photos and create an album that includes detailed descriptions of each photo. Name all

subjects in each photo, along with the events surrounding each snapshot. Imagine those flipping through the album pages are yet to be born.

- What of your possessions will become heirlooms? Select a few of your favorite possessions, anything from jewelry to a well-worn baseball mitt, and designate them as heirlooms, not because of their price tags, but because of their sentimental value. Write about the providence of each of these heirlooms, explaining why they hold such special meaning.
- Create a family time capsule that is filled with genealogy, photographs, sentimental objects, and stories of precious family memories. Make sure multiple generations of your family contribute to the contents of the capsule and agree where it is to be buried and when it should be unearthed. Create a digital document, saved in the cloud that details the contents.

I have 10,700 photos on my iPhone. Ten thousand seven hundred memories I attempted to capture and expect to revisit. When? When is the best time to ignore the present and all the potential it possesses to scroll back in time? Can any of these photos be enough to jog my memory and transport me back to a better place and time? Will the time I spend looking at all these memories be better spent creating new ones? One young father I know bemoaned the fact that he has spent so much time taking pictures of every stage of his baby's life that he doesn't have enough actual memories of moments spent just being present with his son, no camera, just eye contact.

* * *

As I cared for my father during his final decade with dementia, I listened as he spent his days losing and reconfiguring memories. I learned early on that there was no point in correcting or disagreeing. My siblings and I made the conscious decision to avoid starting a sentence with the word *remember*. Visiting with him where he was living in that moment was enough to keep us connected despite his ever-changing reality. It was like a perverse form of time travel, and we were along for the ride.

When he was ninety-two, my dad called and said, "Claire, Claire, I have big news to share." I headed over to his memory care residence to learn that his "big news" was that he had finally decided to quit his job at Motorola—the lifelong career he had retired from twenty-seven years before. He told me he was excited to retire to spend more time with his beautiful Natalie, my mother, who had passed away fifteen years ago. I saw no need to point out her demise as he gazed lovingly at the ornately framed wedding portrait that hung on the wall next to his bed. In that moment he was filled with so much joy and eager anticipation, making new plans that would exit his brain seconds after they entered. But those seconds meant everything to him, and who was I to rob him of this exuberant flash of happiness?

In one of his memory care residences, my dad befriended Susan, a petite, fragile blonde who lived down the hall. They shared every meal together and talked for hours every day. The staff observed them getting closer and closer, and I was touched to find little love notes tucked around his room, hidden in cushions and even in his bathroom medicine cabinet. When they announced they were getting married, the staff were tickled, but they knew better than to start planning the wedding. It was a Groundhog Day sort of affair, with my dad excitedly sharing the big news with me for the first time, every single day.

Susan broke her ankle and went to a rehab facility for three months. When she returned to the memory care floor, neither my dad nor Susan recognized each other and had no interest in reconnecting or even being seated together at meal time. They had no memory of each other or their great romance. It was like being ghosted from a relationship you had no knowledge of.

I was grateful for their courtship, however fleeting, because it filled my dad with giddy joy, something rare and precious in all of our lives, but especially for those stricken with dementia.

* * *

Selective memory is a powerful recircuiting that helps us compartmentalize pain, both mental and physical. In the throes of labor contractions, I was writhing in pain and swearing at the top of my lungs to everyone unlucky enough to be trapped in the room with me that I would never get pregnant again. Then my baby was born, we looked into each other's eyes, snuggled skin to skin, and I suddenly regained my sanity and serenity. My episiotomy miraculously healed and memories of labor and delivery faded, which is why I have two children instead of one.

Does your selective memory help you recall enough happy memories to balance the unhappy ones?

PTSD is a jagged journey that creates psychological and physical manifestations. My dad was a World War II veteran, and, like many of his generation, he had no interest in reminiscing about his time in the military. He shared a few select happy memories just to quell our incessant questions, like how much he liked his job running the movie projector

Are some memories better left unrecovered?

on their Naval aircraft carrier, but we never did get a straight answer about the shrapnel permanently embedded in his leg. His sharing was limited to stories that weren't triggering for him, and we had no choice but to accept that they were enough.

Of course, PTSD strikes many beyond military personnel—affecting about eight million American adults in a given year. Childhood trauma can stay deeply repressed well into adulthood, but not without consequences that can lead to PTSD. I'm well aware of how fortunate I am that, while my childhood had its stumbling blocks, it did not leave residual and debilitating memories, as so often happens with survivors of abuse or neglect.

* * *

If you agree that our memories are what define us as individuals, what can we do to hold on to our memory? How do we keep our brains healthy when we so acutely feel our age in other creaky body parts? "Use it or lose it" sounds cavalier, but this simple recommendation uttered by countless doctors is good advice and enough of a reminder to keep my mind active.

And why not have fun while exercising our brains? Memory games and apps are big business. A quick Google search offers up a whopping 444,000,000 results. These games claim to be developed from neuroscience and cognitive research. BrainHQ offers the mildly snarky marketing slogan, "If you're not using BrainHQ, you're not using your brain." Really? Why don't they just come out and say, "If you don't buy our game, enjoy your slow, heartbreaking decline into dementia"?

When I first heard the term *SuperAger*, I imagined energetic sexagenarians leaping tall buildings despite arthritic knees, and I aspired to be a SuperAger, my long silver hair blowing in the wind just above my voluminous, extremely flattering electric blue superhero cape. In truth, SuperAgers are people over age eighty who have retained the memory capacity typical of middle age. The SuperAging program at Northwestern

University identifies factors that contribute to remarkable memory performance in later life, including genetic, lifestyle, and brain factors. The study collects everything from blood samples to brain scans, cognitive research, and even post-mortem brain donations from the people who sign up for the study. The scientific study of SuperAgers is ultimately a celebration of the aging process, accentuating our potential instead of our decline. SuperAgers are my aspirational role models, giving me yet another reason to look forward to getting older instead of dreading it.

In your most vivid memories, which of your five senses are most often featured?

* * *

I am fascinated by how sensory memories can transport us back to vivid, specific moments in time. Neuroscientists report that when we see, hear, touch, or taste something, that sensory information activates the thalamus, which serves as our cranial air traffic controller, routing the information to the relevant brain areas.

Music can often be the soundtrack for big life memories. For me, The Beatles set the tone, literally, for so many memorable moments. I remember buying my first record at the elementary school book fair. It was a Beatles single with "Do You Want to Know a Secret" on one side and "I Wanna Hold Your Hand" on the other. It was my very first purchase with my own money. I was in first grade, so I hadn't yet discovered the intoxicating thrill of retail therapy. I brought that record home and played it on my pink plastic suitcase record player over and over and over again until it was etched with seismic scratches from the tone arm with the quarter taped on top of it.

Even late in the course of my dad's dementia, when short-term memories moved through his brain as quick as the flutter of a hummingbird's wing, I could put on any, and I mean *any* Frank Sinatra song and he'd start singing along, remembering every word. Frank's lyrics activated a part of my dad's brain that housed happy memories of USO shows, dance halls, and dates with my mom.

In Oliver Sacks' book, *Musicophilia: Tales of Music and the Brain,* the esteemed neuroscientist wrote that he'd seen nonverbal patients with advanced Alzheimer's shiver or weep while listening to music. "Once one has seen such responses," he wrote, "one knows that there is still a self to be called upon, even if music, and only music, can do the calling."

What was playing on the radio the night you got your first kiss? What memories does that song conjure up for you?

For me, no song lyric conjures wistful memories better than "Memories / light the corners of my mind, / misty watercolor memories / of the way we were." Every time I hear that song, I'm right back at the fountain in front of the Plaza Hotel, wishing it were me instead of Barbra Streisand brushing Robert Redford's blond hair out of his eyes.

None of us knows how or when our lives will end, but my parents planned ahead, encouraging us to make our family time together meaningful. They spoke often about making memories. They both donated their bodies to science, eschewing traditional Jewish burials, saying that if we needed a stone to remember them after they were gone, then we probably didn't have enough fun together when they were alive.

TAKE A DEEPER DIVE

How do your childhood memories differ from your siblings' memories?

As one of four children who were born over a span of ten years, I find that my childhood memories, along with my relationship to my parents, are quite different than those of my siblings. Pick a memorable occasion, and see if everyone remembers the same details.

How have memories informed your decision-making?

I grew up in a household of screaming and anger, and because of those memories, I made a conscious choice not to raise my own children that way. What memories influenced your life choices? Make a chart with two columns. In the left column, list impactful memories. In the right column, explain the role each memory played in a subsequent life decision.

***Which of your memories do you most want
to share with the next generation?***

Take some time to reflect on moments that mattered in your life. Write a letter to your loved ones that contains these memories, along with any lessons you learned from them. Include this letter, also called an ethical will, in the file where you keep your will and estate information. Understand that your memories are as precious as any financial bequest or material heirloom.

CHAPTER 17

How Much Is Enough:

L O V E

The Beatles said, "Love is all you need," but I also appreciate my thick, multicolored cashmere scarf on a chilly day, the heady scent of a bouquet filled with lilies and tuberoses, and spontaneous, uncontrollable laugh attacks that have me simultaneously gasping for breath and running to the bathroom.

Don't get me wrong. I'm a huge fan of love. Despite my single status, I believe in love and remain a hopeful romantic. I've been on one dating app or another since my marriage ended with sporadic success. Middle-aged online dating is quite different from "swiping right" in one's twenties. Often I receive a "like" from a man who has totally forgotten that we already went out. It makes me wonder if I'm dealing with his early onset dementia or the utterly underwhelming impression I left on our first date. To be fair, it's probably a combination of both. Twenty-something dates arrive in the same sleek sportscars featured in their profile pics to illustrate their style and prosperity. My sixty-something dates more often than not pick me up in a sedan, proudly displaying their handicap placard like a VIP backstage pass at a concert. Do I believe in love at first sight? Absolutely. But we might have to wait for the Viagra to kick in before consummating that love.

Do you harbor a secret fantasy about the one that got away?

* * *

I thought I knew what forever love was when, at eighteen years old, I got engaged to my college boyfriend after an immediate and passionate attraction. It felt natural, and we both rode the predictable tide of love into marriage, our careers, and then parenthood. Everything seemed to fall into place until my husband's addictions and his erratic behavior made it impossible to stay the course. Our marriage ended after thirty years, and if I am honest, I know that our love died long before we parted ways. When I look back on it, I see it like an inflatable boat, fully buoyant, deftly navigating across the ebbs and flow of our life together. When our love boat sprang its first leaks, we could easily patch them with career successes, beautiful homes, an exotic vacation, the births and milestones of our children. But as time went on and the leaks grew too vast to patch, it became impossible to ignore that all the good in our life wasn't enough to make up for the bad. We were sinking, and I refused to go down with the boat.

Throughout this tumultuous chapter in our lives, I assured my children that they were loved, and I demonstrated this in every way I knew how. Which reminds me once again that love is a verb, not a noun. For me, love is an active and constant pattern of behavior that demonstrates devotion, compassion, and care. I often hear love described as caring more about your loved one's well-being than your own. While I understand the sentiment of this definition, I also see its drawbacks. I am reminded of flight attendants' advice to put your own oxygen mask on first before assisting others. Then again, if the plane is going down, what difference does it really make?

Love is defined in many ways, often with flowery hyperbole that paints love as a grand, all-encompassing life force. One of the most popular definitions of love, 1 Corinthians 13, is often read at weddings. It says, "Love is patient, love is kind. It does not envy, it does not boast, it is not proud. It does not dishonor others, it is not self-seeking, it is not easily angered, and it keeps no record of wrongs. Love does not delight in evil but rejoices with the truth."

Not to sound cynical, but the only time this rang true for me was when I was a delusional twenty-year-old, cinched into my bridal gown, gazing into the eyes of my future husband, under the chuppah, bathed in the candlelight glow of the elegant Lincolnshire Marriott Ballroom, in front of my nearest and dearest. Once the guests left, the candles were extinguished, and the overhead lights snapped back on, the glaring truth was undeniable. Love is a hell of a lot of work, not always patient, often derailed by envy, and displayed boastfully on social media. It may not "dishonor others," but others are often caught in the crossfire of hurt feelings and dashed promises, with wrongs often recorded via texts and emails or in vindictive legal documents. But maybe that's just me.

I believe our understanding of how to give and receive love can be traced back to our childhoods. Despite emotional challenges throughout my own, I always felt love and a sense of belonging to my family. And I was never discouraged to feel my feelings. For as long as I can remember, when I was positively emotionally moved by something, I felt passionately with what I can only describe as love. I have always been the kind of person who dives in headfirst when it comes to expressing my feelings, rarely considering the risks versus the rewards of my actions. And so love comes easily for me. I love my friends, I love my family (most of them, most of the time), and I love many aspects of my life, especially my roles as a parent and now a grandparent. That last one taps into a deep reservoir of love I never knew existed in me. How is it possible to love anyone more than one's own children? Clearly you haven't met my granddaughters.

Have I experienced enough romantic love in my life? Should I be satisfied with my marriage and the two relationships that followed, not expecting more love than I have already received? Am I being greedy? Haven't I had enough romantic adventures for one lifetime?

How much love is enough?

Welcome to my ongoing inner dialogue about love and my work toward accepting what I have today instead of bemoaning what's been lost or what is yet to come. The love I feel from friends, family, and, most importantly, myself really is more than enough to fill me with gratitude.

My daily prayer is this: "God, surround me with love as you see fit." This moment of meditation always gives me an opportunity to reflect on all the love that currently surrounds me. It may not present in the same way romantic love does, but I do believe it has a profound effect on my daily health and serenity.

* * *

At an Al-Anon meeting over a decade ago, I heard a touching expression of love that I've never forgotten. I was newly single. It was a Friday night, and I had no plans, romantic or otherwise. Feeling sorry for myself, I found this meeting nearby and took a seat in the back of the room. Surveying the others, I recognized no one and sunk even deeper into my cushion of self-pity. After the readings and announcements were read, a middle-aged man stood to introduce himself and shared this beautiful story.

My favorite food in the world is Frosted Mini-Wheats. I eat them every day for breakfast. The only thing better is finding that one magnificent mini-wheat that has the absolute perfect ratio of wheat and sugar icing. Those are rare and beautiful things and I always get excited when I find them in my bowl. Today is my birthday, and I received the best gift. My wife is three years sober. When I came home from work today, my beautiful wife was seated at our kitchen table with her reading glasses sliding down her nose. She had tweezers in one hand and was spreading out a huge pile of mini-wheats dumped out of the half-dozen open boxes tilted onto the table with her other hand. She looked up at me with a huge smile and said, "I'm making your birthday present, the ultimate bowl of perfect mini-wheats."

He paused, sat down, and my eyes welled up with tears that flowed well into the next person's share. It was such a profound, clear, simple expression of love that I clearly needed to hear.

* * *

In my early months of being newly single, my dog, Riley, was my loving companion and a constant reminder of how pure love can be. Dogs and other pets love us unconditionally. Learning that having a pet can also reduce the risk of a heart attack was certainly an added bonus. Riley's devotion and unconditional love improved my quality of life and certainly provided enough companionship to combat my loneliness.

In 2015, I read "The 36 Questions That Lead to Love" in *The New York Times* with equal parts skepticism and wonder. Psychologist Arthur Aarons published a study on interpersonal communication that included thirty-six questions, asked and answered in a specific order, that could bring people closer and even potentially accelerate falling in love. After reading about these questions, I proposed this social experiment to the man I was dating. We were still in the early days of falling for each other. Together, we answered these questions thoughtfully and honestly. Questions such as "What would constitute a 'perfect' day for you?" and "If you could change anything about the way you were raised, what would it be?" provided insights into our respective dreams and upbringings. "Is there something that you've dreamed of doing for a long time? Why haven't you done it?" gave me additional understanding of the procrastination tendencies I had already observed in my new beau. "What roles do love and affection play in your life?" gave me

Would you say the presence of an animal created more love in your life? If yes, in what way?

deeper insight into the level of demonstrative love I might expect from him as we grew deeper in love, which we did.

I was grateful for these questions and have not ruled out asking them again should I find myself in a budding new courtship. They provide a template, an emotional icebreaker to get to know someone I'm contemplating giving my whole heart to.

Over thirty years ago, Gary Chapman, a Baptist pastor with a doctorate in adult education, wrote, *The 5 Love Languages: The Secret to Love that Lasts.* He believes that in order to make your partner feel loved, you need to speak that person's "love language." He lists the five most common love languages as (1) words of affirmation, (2) quality time, (3) receiving gifts, (4) acts of service, and (5) physical touch. My love language is an amalgam of all of the above. If you flatter me with compliments and plan exciting dates where you present me with turquoise jewelry while holding my hand, never taking your eyes off me except maybe to jump from your chair to perform the Heimlich maneuver on the choking person at the next table, you are pretty much guaranteed that I'll be your girlfriend.

What Is Your Love Language?

What do you consider your primary "love language"? Touch, words, time, gifts, and acts of service are all outlined in Dr. Gary Chapman's book, *The 5 Love Languages: The Secret to Love That Lasts.* Do you get enough of your desired mode of loving communication? Make a list of some examples of ways you'd like this language communicated. For example, if you would like more touch, list the time, place, and ways touch can be incorporated into your days together. Perhaps suggestions such as starting the day with a good morning hug, holding hands on walks, or ending the day with a goodnight kiss will be warmly received by your partner. Whether or not you are in a relationship, understanding your own love language can help you surround yourself with the kind of love you deserve. Reflect on the list below and complete each sentence with the first thought that resonates with you.

1. My favorite Words of Affirmation are ...
2. An ideal example of Quality Time would be ...
3. I love Receiving Gifts when ...
4. I would define Act of Service as ...
5. Physical Touch comforts me when ...

You may know some couples who got together and lived "happily ever after," but for the rest of us, the kind of love found in fairy tales is unattainable, and notions to the contrary make for a rocky path to love. Fairy tales would have women believe that a prince will rescue us from the perils of everyday life. They also perpetuate the myth that women need to be a certain color, be shaped a certain way, and always wear a gown to be kissed and "saved" by a "prince." That princes have no discernable job or steady income aside from their royal family's trust fund is flat-out worrisome. Let's face it, any man who is content to marry a woman based simply on her shoe size (take note, Cinderella), should be carefully evaluated for mental acuity.

* * *

Many of us know what it feels like to be lovesick, unable to concentrate on anything but our obsessive fantasizing about the one who may or may not in fact be "the one." Lovesickness aside, WebMD reports substantial medical benefits of a loving relationship, which provide compelling inspiration to continue to swipe, I mean, search for your great love. Their data reveals couples in loving relationships have lower blood pressure, fewer colds, and overall better mental health, with less depression, anxiety, and stress. People in loving relationships go to the doctor less often, perhaps because their partner is providing much of the day-to-day diagnosis. The most surprising finding is that a loving relationship provides natural pain control. Maybe that's because no one wants to have sex with a chronic kvetcher, and a regular sex partner who has intimate knowledge of your body is the numero uno social, emotional, and medical benefit of a loving coupling.

Do you believe there is only one great love in each of our lives?

* * *

I want to give a final shout-out for the undeniable power of family love, by birth or by choice. There can never be enough. I believe the family love I give and receive is the reason I am so healthy, both mentally and physically. Thinking about them, caring for them—even from afar—gives me a daily burst of endorphins. I want to end this chapter with a story to illustrate this kind of love.

My son and his girlfriend live in Los Angeles. When they both tested positive for Covid, I felt horrible that, living on the opposite coast, I was unable to help them. I did what any responsible, loving Jewish mother would do. I called Canter's, their favorite local deli, and ordered a large chicken matzo ball soup and two black-and-white cookies to be delivered *stat*. In our family it is common knowledge that chicken soup has magical powers that can cure anything. They received my order within thirty minutes after I heard of their diagnosis. Within five minutes of receiving this delivery, their doorbell rang again, announcing another delivery from Canter's with the exact same order. Had there been a mistake, my son asked? "No sir," the delivery man replied. The first order was sent from Claire and the second order was sent from Jenna. Evidently his sister took the same action I did upon hearing his Covid news, even placing the exact same order I did. In our family there can never be enough love. Or chicken soup.

TAKE A DEEPER DIVE

What's the most memorable example of love you've ever witnessed?

As you contemplate the answer to this question, please think beyond romantic love. Love exists all around us. This question is designed to widen our awareness to find profound love in unlikely places. Can you list ten examples?

Who has made you feel most loved in your life?

People come into our lives for many reasons. Who in your life communicates their love for you most effectively? Write a love letter to them, whether they are dead or alive, and detail all the ways their love has brought you growth, joy, and serenity. This letter is primarily for you, to help you better understand what kinds of love help you thrive in your life.

Do you believe in love at first sight? Have you experienced it?

The answer to this question may not be so simple because love comes in to our lives in so many ways. Perhaps it was the first time you laid eyes on your newborn, or the first time you witnessed a snowfall and tasted a snowflake on your tongue. Give this question some thought before answering, either on paper or in conversation.

CHAPTER 18

How Much Is Enough:

S E X

A note to my readers: This chapter is about celebrating sex positivity. I am not going to address sexual assault or sexual harassment in this chapter, and not because I don't recognize it as important or relevant. I'm not going to address it because it can be triggering for those who have been victimized, and that is never my intention with any of my writing. I hope this chapter will only bring you joy and serve as a playful opportunity to ask yourself if you are enjoying your body enough, with or without a partner.

Is your sex life one of wonder or regret? My sexuality has much to do with my self-awareness and self-esteem. I have learned to love my body enough from the inside out thanks in no small part to generous, body-positive partners.

I have a dear friend in her seventies who looks back on her life with great satisfaction. She's raised two exceptional children on her own. She's had great career success that came with an impressive income. She had a comfortable amount of fame, more flattering than intrusive. She's truly beautiful inside and out, and she's in good health. She has deep, meaningful friendships, many of which span multiple decades. She has just one regret: she wishes she'd had more sex.

> **How much is enough sex for you to feel positively connected to your body?**

I was not raised to perceive my sexuality as social currency. There were no conversations about sex in my childhood home, and I rarely observed a *come hither* gaze between my mother and father. It wasn't until I was in high school that I came to understand sex appeal as an alluring form of self-marketing. Observing the perky cheerleaders pursue the varsity football players with such measured focus fascinated me. I watched them stalk their prey by altering their walks, increasing their giggles, and deepening their voices. Their clothes seemed to fit just a little tighter, and their coquettish demeanor would inevitably turn the guys' heads. From my perspective, it was like watching Pamela Anderson teach a flirting masterclass. I viewed this as women having power over men, and I wanted to know more.

How has your attitude about sex changed as you've gotten older?

Sexual wellness was not taught, promoted, or even contemplated during my budding adolescence. There was no booming commerce surrounding sexual health like we have today. I had no access to companies like Gwyneth Paltrow's Goop and their Sexual Wellness package that includes two "pleasure essentials": a bottle of a dietary supplement that supports a woman's sexual desire, libido, and mood, and an ultra-plush, self-heating, curved G-spot vibrator, which would have come in handy in my twenties as I had absolutely no idea that I had a G-spot, no clue where it might be located, and no understanding of what it was for. In my thirty years of marriage, my husband never located my G-spot.

If you are a parent, do you feel you did a good enough job teaching your children about sex? Did your parents give you enough information regarding your sex education?

Post-divorce, I was ecstatic to learn that I did indeed have a navigable G-spot. I welcomed its presence in my nether regions. I flung the doors open. Every new lover is welcome to explore and delight.

Despite what most women have been told, I have come to believe that love is not necessary to have great sex. Love may deepen the emotional aspect of sex for some, but for others, the less emotional attachment, the better the *wham-bam.*

No strings attached, Netflix and Chill, Friends with Benefits, Roll in the Hay, Getting It On, Boinking, DTF, Shagging, and—my favorite—*Schtupping* are all popular slang terms for sex. And regardless of age, it is enough for both men and women to simply enjoy sex for the sake of pure pleasure and release, without promises of anything else.

Way back in 1973, Erica Jong coined the phrase "zipless fuck" in her best seller, *Fear of Flying.* I remember reading this book in high school. It was my first introduction to the joy of sex without love or commitment. I find it immensely exciting that a new generation of women are now reading her groundbreaking novel. It has resonated with over twenty million readers since its first publication. Her creative sexual content like, "Zippers fell away like rose petals, underwear blew off in one breath like dandelion fluff," really astounded me. Pure pleasure could be enough. Relationships were optional. Fifty years later, with the pervasiveness of dating apps, I'm happy to report that consensual, casual sex is as commonplace for women as for men, with much less judgment. Unless you are in Mike Pence's family, in which case you probably have a high feminist mountain to climb.

Of course, casual sex with a partner isn't the only path to arousal. Solo sexual fantasies can be enough to satisfy many people in or out of partnership. Some appreciate visual aids like porn, while others turn to erotica or romance novels to get in the mood. Porn is not for me, but not for the reasons you may think. I usually spend too much time critiquing the cinematic aspects, such as poor lighting, improbable plot progression, and bad acting, to become aroused. I enjoy erotic literature, but simultaneously balancing a book, wearing my prescription glasses, and working my vibrator is logistically problematic.

During the Covid pandemic, fear of physical contact and the isolation of lockdown had many of us shelling out serious money for sexual satisfaction. Researchandmarkets.com's *2022 Sex Toys—Global Market Trajectory & Analytics* reports the global market for sex toys totaled $35.1 billion in 2020 and is projected to reach $58.6 billion by 2027.

This healthy change in attitudes makes me smile. More and more millennial couples are now adding sex toys to their bridal registries, making gifting oh so much more entertaining. Why not throw a cock ring in with your napkin rings? How about a dildo with the dishware? Maybe a vibrator with the vacuum?

I and many women I know are big fans of vibrators for solo pleasure. It's an important tool for learning the terrain of our own bodies and locating erogenous zones that may have been ignored through conventional sex. I think it's great that more people are less hesitant about discussing masturbation and sharing tips and toy suggestions with friends, further demystifying and celebrating our sexuality. How would you know about Moon Juice Sex Dust or Dame Arousal Serum if it weren't for a helpful in-the-know pal? And, just between us, how many vibrator-induced orgasms are enough? That's for you to decide.

I owe a debt of gratitude to my friends in the LGBTQ community for their candor, ease, and sense of humor surrounding sex play. I admire and learn from my lesbian and bi-sexual pals' unselfconscious approach and open-hearted communication surrounding physical intimacy. I envy sexual fluidity. Being able to feel attraction to both men and women would give me so many more options, but unfortunately, I am just not wired that way.

Have you ever felt shame for using sex toys, thinking that purchasing and using them meant that you or your partner alone wasn't enough?

The Downside of (Social) Lubrication

Do you need alcohol or drugs to muster up enough confidence to enjoy uninhibited sex? Unfortunately, "social lubrication" is a misnomer for alcohol when combined with sex. For men in particular, alcohol and recreational drugs may have negative complications that accompany perceived confidence and release of inhibitions. Reported complications include erectile dysfunction, reduced libido, and problems with both orgasms and ejaculation. Here are some ways to enjoy sex without social lubrication:

1. Change of scenery. Head to the great outdoors to find a private setting in nature. Prefer to stay indoors? Travel to different rooms in your home for sexual adventures outside the bedroom.
2. Role play. Explore your fantasies through dialogue and/or costume. Perhaps a fantasy scenario might include your brawny repairman or Amazon delivery person. Take this as far as all participants consent to.
3. Toys. Without judgment or recrimination, have fun and deepen your pleasure by introducing new sex toys into your romantic repertoire.

One of my challenges in the dating world is that I do not drink alcohol. Unfortunately, many men see this as a sexual impediment. Most of my dates enjoy the lubricating powers of alcohol to shed inhibitions and get the party started. I have no need for that sort of lubrication. Other kinds of lubricant, yes—hello, I'm in my sixties—but, with the right partner, I can have a great time in bed without consciousness-altering substances.

I found this out the hard way early in my newly single life when a well-intentioned suitor offered me an edible as we headed out for our first date. I admit I was curious. We were splitting one, and it was so tiny that I was confident I could handle it. A half hour later as we ordered dinner, I was riveted by his intense, palpable charisma. Our conversation flowed effortlessly, and he was hands down the smartest, sexiest, most fascinating man I had ever gone out with. We laughed at each other's jokes. The chemistry felt electric. We enjoyed our dinner, and I looked forward to bringing him back to my house and having him for dessert. As we walked back to my apartment, I could feel a shift in our energy. Our pace slowed and the laughter was more subdued. I welcomed him in with a passionate kiss. We headed to the bedroom and got comfy in my bed. Perhaps too comfy. Both of us burrowed in the blankets and immediately started nodding off, too high even for foreplay. As I drifted off to sleep I felt frustrated at how quickly our energy shifted. It was a missed opportunity that I've replayed often in my mind. How much is enough-but-not-too-much edible cannabis is probably the biggest challenge for many users.

I made a promise to myself when I became single at fifty that I would never apologize for any part of my body as I contemplated getting naked for new partners. Now sixty-six, I can say that I have kept that promise to myself, and, even better, have been with men who loved every soft curve they laid their hands on. I have learned to appreciate so much about my body through their touch, and I feel incredibly grateful for my middle-life awakening. One extremely gifted lover admitted to me that he prefers the intimate company of larger women because he finds them to be less self-conscious and more open to having fun in bed. Who am I to argue?

I pray for a world where love is love and sex is sex—a world where, as consenting adults, we could have any kind of sex with whomever we wanted without fear of judgment from family, church, downstairs neighbors, or government intervention. What a wonderful world that would be.

TAKE A DEEPER DIVE

How does your age impact your sex life?

There's a common misconception that a woman's sex drive diminishes as she ages. I contend that it's not the sex drive, it's the adoration, enthusiasm, and skill of her partner that diminishes. Do you agree? Write an essay just for you that tracks the way your sexual prowess, energy, and interest have changed as you've aged. This essay will become a treasured document that charts an intimate part of your life.

In your opinion, are you open enough about your sexuality?

Many people seem to be uncomfortable discussing sex. Much of this discomfort stems from how sexuality was or wasn't discussed in the families we were raised in. When and where did you acquire your comfort level? From whom did you receive the best information about sex?

Do you feel you have had enough "casual" sex?

Some people equate casual sex with promiscuity. Others see it as a proclamation of independence and self-exploration.

Write a letter to yourself on the topic of casual sex. Talk about your conquests, or lack thereof, and your feelings about them. Without any judgment, reflect on the role casual sex did or did not play in your life journey.

CHAPTER 19

How Much Is Enough:

R E L I G I O N

Is religion a constant, integral part of your life? As I've gotten older, the lines between spirituality, activism, and religion have blurred. I struggle with this and often ask myself how much of each is enough for me to feel centered.

At this point in my life, I have less interest in organized religion and, I suppose, less need for it. I was raised in a very reform Jewish home, and because we moved around so much, our family never had enough time to establish roots within any one Jewish community. Neither of my parents was deeply religious, so we rarely lit Sabbath candles and celebrated only the big holidays, especially the ones with special meals and gifts. While our religious observance may seemed laissez-faire, and some fellow temple members perceived us to be not Jewish enough, my mom drew the line at Christmas decorations. No tree would be installed or adorned in our home, and my mom balked at the concept of a Chanukah bush. As a child, I pushed back on her edict, not wanting to celebrate for its religious meaning, just for its ornate decor. I found an ideal workaround: I made my Barbies gentile and bought a Christmas tree for their Dream House, which made my mom laugh and relent.

My kids were raised as members of a historic synagogue with inspiring community engagement, great summer camps, hip rabbis, and relevant ideology. Even so, when they were young, they too asked for a Christmas tree. I had grown comfortable just celebrating Chanukah and told them when they had their own homes they could decorate them for the holidays any way they chose. Sure enough, once they were on their own, they decorated their homes for both Christmas and Chanukah, putting up Christmas trees with twinkling lights as well as menorahs holding twisty, old-school Chanukah candles that dripped colorful wax all over every flat surface. When queried today, both kids say they are Jewish, giving me enough confidence to know I raised them with a spiritual identity. The rest is really up to them. Religious beliefs are so personal, so individualized, and ever-changing based on our own life circumstances. As a parent of fully grown adults, I believe I'm doing enough just living my life by example.

I meet a lot of adults who say they are lapsed Catholics. I've also met both Christians and Jews who feel the organized religion they were born into rejects a fundamental aspect of their current lifestyle, making it difficult to embrace their doctrine. I had my own distasteful brush with this sort of religious rejection when my rabbi, who had known my children since they were very young, told me he wouldn't officiate my daughter's nuptials because she was marrying outside the faith. This felt like a boot swiftly kicking my tush out the literal synagogue door with a finality that furthered my conviction that "holier than thou" attitudes have no place in my life.

* * *

There are priests, pastors, and rabbis who work hard to stay current and inclusive, and there are also those who are unbending, stubbornly clinging to tradition even at the expense of losing new generations of congregants challenged by an ever-changing world.

I'm impressed with pastors like Jane Voigts, who adopts an engaging, entertaining approach to religious leadership thanks to her previous career in comedy and improv. Jane even created "The Bible Cabaret," an evening of playful exploration of biblical texts in the form of a variety show. Jane says, "The Bible is a collection of stories that were meant to entertain as well as enlighten and inspire. And, the Bible takes the command to 'rejoice always' seriously, because its contents are, primarily, comedy!"

Jane is currently the pastor of the United Methodist Church in Palm Springs, California, where she reads her congregants the way stand-ups read their audiences. She inspires and connects through her engaging, inclusive sermons. She believes you can never have too much fun on the pulpit, and, as a bonus, she's quite the fashion plate. Jane's earned a glamorously kitchy reputation throughout Palm Springs for her eclectic collection of mid-century pantsuits and caftans.

* * *

Pointing to a religious rule gives parents a spiritual copilot, perhaps even someone to blame when their children challenge their belief system. "Hey, I didn't make the rules. God did!"

I think it's natural for us to question our religious identity at some point in our lives, even at the risk of being rejected, or even worse, cast off by family members. My parents were never heavy-handed about Judaism, and I felt free to explore the meaning of my own faith, BLT sandwich in hand.

At any point in your life, did you question if your religion was enough of a pathway to living a spiritual life?

The Amish offer a great compromise with *Rumspringa*, where, starting around the age of sixteen, Amish youth are given permission to explore activities normally shunned by their faith, including going to the movies, drinking alcohol, wearing non-Amish apparel, and participating in organized sports. The hope is that their expanded social life will give them enough of a glimpse into the complications and moral struggles of the outside world to find their way back to their Amish life, ideally with a partner who shares the Amish tenets. Rumspringa officially ends with a church baptism, signaling a permanent commitment to the Amish religion.

Often, one person can be enough to profoundly change another's spiritual life path through religious education and compassionate guidance. As a young child living in Benin, West Africa, my brother-in-law Gilbert was sent by his parents to live with relatives on the other side of the country who needed help farming their land. Benin is a desperately poor country with few opportunities for employment or education. Gilbert's relatives promised Gilbert an advanced education in exchange for his labor , but the arrangement made him feel very much alone and unloved, like an indentured servant. He found comfort in the local Catholic church, where Father Michel Loiret's encouragement helped him begin to feel optimistic about his future. For Gilbert, religious guidance provided enough enlightenment to guide him toward a better life.

* * *

Like many people, I've engaged in meaningful discussions with religious leaders about the presence of God in the world, hoping they could provide enough comfort and insight to mitigate my fear or uncertainty with something I was struggling with. I had a life-changing conversation with Rabbi Paul. A dear friend of mine gave birth to a child with a chronic, debilitating illness for which there is no cure, and I asked Rabbi Paul how God could let a child be born with a lifelong medical challenge and such a precarious future. He said, and I am quoting directly here, "Shit happens." He explained that I was searching for God in the wrong place. "God is not the cause of the bad in the world," he explained; "God can be found in the love and support that *surrounds* the bad in the world." In the case of my friend's child, God was to be found in the devotion of the parents, friends, and medical professionals who would surround the child with compassionate care. Similarly, he said, "God is not behind natural disasters,

For you, is religion spiritual or cultural or both? Do you feel you have enough of a spiritual or religious presence in your life?

political unrest, or criminal activity but in the dedication of public servants along with private citizens and their commitment to be of service to others." This totally shifted my understanding of God as a higher power and provided me with more than enough insight to see my role in my ever-evolving spiritual life.

* * *

I aspire to be like the religious activists who have figured out the ideal balance between thought and action. And while I have no interest in becoming a nun—no surprise there—I have deep admiration for the nuns featured in the 2021 documentary film *Rebel Hearts*. Lenore Dowling, now in her nineties, was one of the Sisters of the Immaculate Heart of Mary, who gained notoriety in the 1960s for bucking the rigid, conservative life dictated by the archbishop of Los Angeles. They used their platform as spiritual educators to teach activism by example. The Sisters empowered each other, and generations of students, to stand up for what they believed in despite persistent pushback from the Catholic church. "They thought they could bury us, but they didn't know we were seeds," says Rosa Manriquez, who attended Sisters of the Immaculate Heart schools and was inspired by their example to a life of activism.

Sister Simone Campell, a nun and attorney, is another Catholic who would be in my spiritual leadership Hall of Fame if I had one. Civil rights protests during the 1960s moved her deeply. "The gospel spoke to me," she says of that time, and she resolved to combine her faith with activism for the cause of equality. As executive director of the lobbying group Network, Campbell launched a campaign called "Nuns on the Bus" in 2012 to protest social and financial inequality across the country. Though Network was condemned by the Vatican as a "bad influence," Campbell and her fellow nuns felt enough of a duty to their spiritual truth to stand up to the church and continue to spread their message.

We've all heard more than enough examples of the misinterpretation and misuse of religion in pursuit of power. I hope we can all agree that there is no place for prejudice, violence, or abuse in the name of religion.

I'm fascinated by people who find or convert to a new religion later in life. I certainly understand the ongoing search for a deeper meaning in one's life, but how and when do you know that the religion you were raised with is not enough of a spiritual fit for your lifestyle today? Public Religion Research Institute (PRRI) is a nonprofit, nonpartisan organization specializing in "research at the intersection of religion, values, and public life." A recent PRRI study revealed that approximately sixty-four million Americans—that's one in five—identify as "spiritual but not religious," also known as SBNR. Many people interviewed for the study had left the religion they were raised in but still believed in a power greater than themselves.

If you left the faith in which you were raised, when did you realize you no longer belonged there?

I connect with my spirituality through meditation, nature, yoga, and Twelve Step affiliations. For me, organized religion is simply not enough to encompass my spiritual belief system. In fact, it is often in conflict with my spiritual life.

Both my children had a Bar and Bat Mitzvah, a deeply spiritual rite of passage from childhood into adulthood. Both kids worked hard to learn their Torah portion and all the prayers and rituals surrounding this seminal event. I told both of them that after their Bar and Bat Mitzvahs they could choose their own religious and/or spiritual path. I felt strongly that they should complete this chapter of their Jewish studies, and despite some pushback, I am confident that they now look back on their Bar and Bat Mitzvah as an important religious ritual. Aside from a wedding ceremony, there are few events in life where all your friends and family surround you for no reason other than to provide love and support and celebrate your accomplishments. These events, along with the abundant buffets that usually accompany them, are truly memorable.

Yes, Bar and Bat Mitzvah parties are fun, but we did not go overboard. Our receptions were held at the synagogue directly following the service, without elaborate decor or expense to distract from the true meaning of the day. My son's centerpieces were towers of canned soup that were donated to the temple food pantry at the conclusion of the party—a gentle reminder to all in attendance that community service was very much a part of our religious practice.

Learn About Other Religions

Learning about religions other than your own can be an enlightening personal journey that may bridge social divides, bring you closer to your own faith, or lead you on a different spiritual path. Some ways to expand your spiritual awareness:

1. Attend services outside your faith to deepen your spiritual sense of community.
2. Read about other religions beside your own for a better understanding of the spiritual practices that exist in the world.
3. Create your own religion that best suits your personal spiritual practice and beliefs.

Ironically, I never struggled more with my Jewish identity than the decade when I was employed as the communications director for the preschool at a conservative synagogue. I had just gotten divorced and needed to find a job that offered a steady paycheck and insurance benefits. As a comedian, I knew I had expertise as a communicator, and I love children, so this felt like something I could do to earn a living while still pursuing my creative ambitions. Little did I know that getting up close and personal with religion as an employee would challenge me spiritually. I grew weary listening to the trio of rabbis' constant discord over different interpretations of Judaism, leaving me confused, disenfranchised, and convinced that the three different Jewish branches—reform, conservative, and orthodox—were more like three different religions, none of which felt like an ideal spiritual fit for me.

Clearly many of my fellow citizens who walk peacefully and purposefully get their spiritual needs met by means other than organized religion. Perhaps we can even draw a parallel between religious orientation and restaurant dining. We can order the Tasting Menu and receive what the chef recommends, or we can order à la carte, picking and choosing what sounds good to us. And of course, many spiritual seekers opt for the all-you-can-eat buffet, where we just throw ourselves wholeheartedly, indiscriminately into the mix. And we can always choose vegetarian or vegan options, the agnostic and atheist versions of haute cuisine.

I respect agnostics—those who neither believe nor disbelieve in God—because they aren't afraid to ask the hard questions. They also admit to not having all the answers, which is a sign of intelligence in my book—because does anyone really have all the answers? I may in fact be an agnostic Jew. Even though I was raised Jewish, had a Bat Mitzvah, married a Jewish man, raised my kids in a Jewish home, and worked in a synagogue for ten years, my understanding of Judaism and its role in my current life is ambiguous at best, which begs the question, "Am I Jewish enough?"

Atheists seem to have enough grounding and self-assuredness not to need enlightenment from a higher power. Perhaps they innately possess answers to the big questions many of us struggle to answer. Or maybe they were just raised to believe that religion is an optional accessory, like an in-dash GPS system in a car. Handy, but not essential for a well-navigated life.

Today, my family celebrate Chanukah, Christmas, Easter, and Passover. Rosh Hashanah and December 31st both usher in our new year. When we're looking for a taste of religion, we just break out the bagels. Because a fresh-from-the-oven everything bagel topped with cream cheese and Russ & Daughters hand-sliced smoked salmon is enough of a religious experience to satisfy our entire family.

Can you imagine a world without religion? What would it look and feel like? If there were no religion, do you believe the world would be at peace?

In this chapter, I've focused on the religions I have the greatest familiarity with. Whether you are Christian, Jewish, Muslim, Hindu, Buddhist, or any other religion, the questions below are designed to prompt further contemplation.

TAKE A DEEPER DIVE

Do you believe that most organized religions offer enough of an ethical template for every age and stage of life?

Write about the role organized religion has played in your life. What positive aspects of your character do you attribute to having grown up with, or without, organized religion?

Do you consider yourself religious enough? If yes, how does religion define you? If no, do you have another spiritual practice?

I remember the time in my childhood when I became aware that my family's religion was just one of many. I wondered about how everyone chooses their religion. To this day, I am fascinated by all the ways we pick and choose the parts of our religion that work best for us. Do you think that embracing only certain aspects of our religion make us religious enough? Write about the ways your religion or other spiritual practice touches your life.

*Who in your life incorporates enough spirituality
to inspire your own personal growth?*

List your religious and/or spiritual role models. They need
not be religious leaders; your list could include coworkers,
friends, family members, a musician, or an author. Write
about the qualities you admire in each and the valuable
life lessons you learned through their examples.

CHAPTER 20

How Much Is Enough:

M O N E Y

grew up in a middle-class home where my dad was the sole breadwinner who often expressed anger and frustration at the cost of raising four children. My mother did the best she could to stretch a dollar, putting starchy, inexpensive food on the table and dressing us all in hand-me-downs that were simultaneously threadbare from too much laundering and thick with the mending and patching from too many playground scuffles. These cost-cutting efforts were rarely acknowledged or appreciated by my father. Money was a huge source of stress in our home.

Do you believe there is such a thing as enough money?

As I observed my stay-at-home mother's financial dependence on my father and their constant aggressive arguing over money, I vowed I would be financially independent when I grew up. The feeling that there was never enough money kept my mother on edge and served to further exacerbate her already fragile mental health. The angry conversations and worry over money were oppressive and often felt punitive, as if we children were all to blame for how expensive we were to maintain. I distinctly remember hearing my parents say, "What do you mean, those shoes are too small? We just bought them for you last month. Stop growing so fast!"

Now, as an adult reflecting back on my childhood, I realize that indeed there was enough money. We were all fed and cared for, and we all graduated college with no debt thanks to my parents' frugality. I appreciated the privilege of starting my adult life debt-free, and my sense of awe and admiration became even deeper after I had the experience of budgeting to pay for my own kids' education. I know everyone is not so lucky. I have a friend who wasn't able to pay off her college loans until she was in her fifties. That debt felt like a fussy child strapped to her back, always hungry, crying to be fed, and never receiving enough to be satisfied.

The concept of what constitutes "enough" money is highly personal, and the issue sometimes becomes competitive, which can leave us in a vulnerable state of mind. My father retired after thirty-four years of dedicated employment, and my parents lived comfortably off his company pension and life savings until their deaths. By all appearances, my father was a success, and his earnings served our family admirably. I wish he had known and felt that throughout our childhoods. I wish there could have been enough faith in our future to replace the financial stress of our past.

Is it possible to be considered successful without great wealth?

* * *

At what point in our lives do we begin defining success in dollars and cents? When my children started earning an allowance and had accumulated around ten dollars, I offered them a trip to the local toy store. As we walked the aisles stacked floor-to-ceiling with enticing options, I often challenged them to think about spending versus saving their allowance. They'd excitedly hold up a toy, and I'd bust out my best game show host voice and announce, "Yes, you have enough money to buy that doll!" Then, conjuring my inner Vanna White, I would say,

"But wait! If you save double this amount, you would have enough to buy that doll and"—here I would point with a dramatic swoop—"her BRAND NEW CAR!" The decision was always theirs because I felt it was the process, not just the prize, that would plant the seeds for their financial success.

Since my kids managed their pocket money from a young age, they were constantly weighing the concept of *enough*. "Do I have enough?" "Have I saved enough?" And, my personal favorite because it showed initiative, "What do I need to do to get more?"

I was a mom on a mission. I mounted a poster on our family bulletin board that had a line drawn horizontally through the middle. Attached to this poster was a pouch full of colorful stickers. When the kids completed a chore, did their homework without complaint, or initiated an act of kindness without a prompt, they'd get to put a stamp above the line. If they acted out, got in trouble at school, didn't keep their room clean, or were impolite or uncaring toward a family member, they'd get a stamp below the line. At the end of the week we would count up the stamps, and if there were more stamps above the line than below it, they'd receive more allowance. I caught both kids several times each week checking that poster to see how they were doing, and I believe it helped them make better decisions without my having to scold or harangue. Or maybe that is just wishful thinking on my part. Now adults, they both vividly remember the poster and all the "You're gonna get a stamp below the line if you do that" taunts they would toss at each other just for spite.

Fast-forward twenty-five years. Both kids are now independent, financially secure, thirty-somethings who love their jobs, which, in itself, is enough of a reason for all of us to feel successful. Whew. My work here is done.

Or is it?

These days I'm entertained by the financial musings of my five-year-old granddaughter, Natalie. She is aware that an ATM will spit out money when you push certain buttons. So when I say I don't have enough money to buy some toy, balloon, stuffie, or treat she's begging for, she tells me just to go to the money machine. I tell her it doesn't quite work that way, that I have to put in money to get out money. She asks how I get money, and I tell her that I earn it. The concept of earning money is still too abstract for her to grasp, so the conversation usually ends with an impassioned plea for ice cream.

* * *

My financial advisor, Andrea, credits her grandmother for teaching her about friendship and money in one fell swoop. "When I was very young, Mom-Mom—as we called her—used to say, 'People are like money. Over the years you collect your coins, and every penny counts. You will one day meet your silver dollar, and you and your spouse will find friends who are your half-dollar coins. Now, a really wealthy person also has quarters, which are friends from childhood, work, charities you've been involved with. They will be there for you thick and thin. Most everyone else in life are dimes, people you see regularly but don't have deep, meaningful conversations with. Nickels and pennies are acquaintances that you say hello to in passing. Don't discard the pennies, as one day they may become dimes.'"

How old were you when you first spent your own money?

It's no surprise that Andrea grew up to be a successful bookkeeper, accountant, and financial advisor. And a half-dollar friend.

* * *

Can money buy happiness? Jack and Jewell Whittaker's quick answer to that question would be a resounding *no*. They owned a sewer pipe-laying business when, in 2002, Jack won $314 million, the largest undivided lottery jackpot in history. Jack vowed he would donate millions to launch a charitable foundation. Sadly, his foundation was targeted by scammers and forced to suspend operations the following year.

Jack's reputation rapidly diminished as he paid frequent raucous visits to the local strip club, flashing ridiculous amounts of cash and harassing the female employees. Tragically, the Whittakers' financially indulged granddaughter spiraled into drug addiction and went missing. About two years after Jack bought that winning Powerball ticket, police found her body dumped behind a van. Jack's wife, Jewell, blamed the Powerball jackpot for destroying their family. "I wish I would have torn that ticket up," she told a Charleston newspaper reporter.

This is not a trick question: Does money buy happiness?

My comedy career in the 1980s was pretty much the opposite of winning the lottery. It meant working on the road in comedy clubs for very little money, jockeying for the prime spot on a lineup in hopes I might be spotted by a manager or agent who might get me an audition for *Saturday Night Live* or maybe a coveted stand-up slot on a popular late night show, with about the same odds as winning the lottery.

If you won a big lottery jackpot, what would you do with the prize money?

I've been fortunate to have financially advantageous years in comedy, but I never craved fame, and I made conscious choices to forgo pivotal career moves that would have certainly brought in more money. I opted for more time with my family. Toilet training instead of a *Tonight Show* gig? Yes, and I have no regrets.

* * *

Like most working parents, I struggled with the precarious balancing act of career and family. It seemed there were never enough hours in the day to excel at both, and I remain in awe of my friends who figured out how to do it. My friend Jill had great success as a television producer. Most days were long and hyper-focused with enormous responsibilities. To the outsider, Jill had the dream life in show business, filled with celebrities, awards shows, and critical acclaim. Jill's career was a real-life Hollywood success story. Who could ask for anything more?

What role does money play in your definition of success?

Jill loved her work. She felt destined to be married to her career rather than a partner, but once Jill got married and became a parent, she began to rethink her work-life balance. She shared the day she had her epiphany and recognized she had enough of her precarious balancing act.

What career would you choose (or have chosen) if you were independently wealthy?

"I was deep in a TV production meeting and my phone lit up with a picture of my son frolicking in a field at a local farm, where he was joyfully plucking produce, enjoying a beautiful, sunshine-filled day with his nanny. At that exact moment, my priorities shifted dramatically. I realized I wanted to spend my days in that field with my son.

"And within weeks of leaving my job and spending more dedicated time with him, my son blossomed. His school was closed due to the pandemic, so we started doing homework together as part of our daily activities to have some form of structure. He started to read, write, and do math at four years old. I'm forever grateful for how we taught each other. This precious opportunity is one I would have missed if I had continued to spend my days at the office, and that realization has cracked my heart wide open."

Jill shared this additional personal reflection: "Sometimes 'enough' doesn't mean feeling full and then disconnecting from everything you have built or worked for, but rather just finding your pivot. So experiencing 'enough' of one person, place, or purpose can allow space for you to shift your energy and passion into something else."

* * *

Many would argue that until you actually have enough money, you really don't have the luxury of questioning how much money is indeed *enough*. How does the concept of *enough* factor into the decision many have to make between feeding their families or paying rent?

I was blissfully ignorant about money until I started earning some. No one taught me about spending versus saving for my future. I never took a class on financial management. I vividly remember opening my first checking account in college and not having a clue what a checkbook was for. *Am I supposed to be writing something in there? What exactly am I supposed to be adding and subtracting on these long, lined pages?* Balancing my checkbook was as foreign to me back then as it is now, because who even uses a checkbook anymore? I really wish I would have had the opportunity to learn about managing my money without being embarrassed or ashamed of how little I knew.

Susan Yeagley and Galia Gichon are the hosts of *The Fiscal Firecrackers*, a popular *Money Meets Funny* podcast that educates, entertains, and empowers listeners to be smarter with their money. If only I'd had access to this podcast in college, my finances and my self-esteem would have been very different.

On a recent episode, Galia made my heart skip a beat when she said, "Know your worth, and not just in financial terms." As a financial educator, she often stresses that it's the habits, not the number of zeros in your bank balance, that define your financial success. "I never say, 'You have enough' to my clients. That's not for me to say." Both Susan and Galia agree that money matters are highly personal and that, for many people, talking about money can be more uncomfortable than talking about sex.

> **Did you receive enough financial education? Who was your guide?**

* * *

If only we had a way to make and save enough money while having fun. My friend Jeff has a career that is the envy of many. He's a professional gambler. I've observed people swarm him at dinner parties, as if just being in close proximity will give them the secrets he possesses.

Jeff knew he was good at math at a young age. He declared mathematics as his major at Northwestern University and graduated with the same goal of every other graduate: get a job and make money. He held uninspiring traditional jobs until he was twenty-six, while always enjoying some recreational gambling. Soon he realized he could earn a living gambling, but had serious doubts about making it his career.

Jeff finally decided to quiet the skeptical voice in his head and pursue what he loved: a full-time career in gambling. Accepting that what he was doing was illegal did not deter him, despite the fact he had grown up being a 'good boy' and was proud of his ethical, law-abiding behavior his entire life.

All went well until Jeff spent his thirty-fifth birthday in jail after Chicago Vice Squad discovered his sports betting business from phone records. Their search warrant was ruled illegal, so all charges were dropped, and Jeff promptly moved to Las Vegas, where his work had no criminal ramifications. He threw himself into blackjack, video poker, and even a progressive Keno game, where three months of dedicated play netted him a jackpot of $234,000. His new girlfriend—and now wife—was with Jeff when he won. Talk about the ultimate first date score. Not long after the Keno windfall, they hit a stunning $100,000 video poker win. Both realized Jeff's analytical approach to gambling was no flash in the pan.

To augment his income from casino gambling, Jeff partnered with another local pro on a computer-generated baseball betting business that provided enough steady income to span fifteen years, well into Jeff's years as a husband and father.

How does a professional gambler know he's made or lost enough? Jeff explains, "My whole career is one long series of mathematical judgements. When those equations no longer make sense and my advantage is gone, I walk away." And though he may make enough from one particular game, he knows there will always be another. And another. Jeff has no interest in retiring or quitting the profession he's come to love.

Now a healthy, happy sixty-seven-year-old, married for twenty-six years and the father of two adult sons, Jeff hesitates when I ask him if he considers himself to be successful. When Jeff first moved to LA, he rubbed shoulders with wealthier neighbors and friends, and it made him question whether he was earning enough for his family. He and his wife own a house in an affluent Los Angeles suburb, put their sons through private school and college, and traveled extensively on annual family adventures.

Is loving what you do as, or more important than, the money you earn?

Jeff says, "I know what my wife and I have is enough, but I sometimes struggle with falling into the trap of wanting more because my neighbors appear to have so much more."

* * *

Most of my sixty-something friends are staring down the next chapter of life that may include retirement, a fixed income, and less definition of self through career achievements. Will they still consider themselves successful when they no longer draw a steady paycheck, sign their name with their impressive job title, or enjoy the perks that accompany a generous expense account?

My baby brother, Bob, retired at sixty. That line makes me laugh every time I read it. How could that little, restless kid I grew up with complete thirty-seven successful years in a high-powered position at one of the nation's biggest accounting firms? He had a demanding job, and he traveled extensively, overseeing operations for all the company's offices. To be financially prepared, he started saving early so he would have enough money to retire young. Bob's financial advisor gave him enough confidence when he assured Bob and my sister-in-law that their money would last well into their nineties.

Does the Idea of Retirement Scare or Excite You?

One thing I know for sure: we are all getting older, and if we are fortunate enough to reach retirement age, at some point we will have to decide if we want to keep working indefinitely or retire and start a whole chapter of life. Take a sheet of paper and divide it in two columns. On one side write Pro, and on the other, Con. Reflect on your personal and professional life, and under each column list the pros and cons of retirement as they apply to your life. Having both written down on one sheet will give you a much more balanced view of what lies ahead.

Unlike my brother Bob, I am not ready to retire. I feel like I am just getting started on a new chapter of life, a much less flashy chapter, where money, status, and stuff hold far less importance than they used to. I am proof that money doesn't buy happiness, and Harvard University backs me up. Their business school surveyed 818 millionaires and discovered that "even individuals with a net worth of ten million dollars think they need to increase their wealth dramatically to be happier." I feel validated in my belief that happiness is a conscious state of mind, not a big fat bank account.

I just closed the books on my year-end financials and discovered that I made less money in 2022 than in any previous year in my forty-plus year career. And yet, I have never felt more successful, more at peace, and more proficient at achieving a rewarding work-life balance. I've given up major material possessions, including my own home and my car, to move into my daughter and son-in-law's building to help care for their kids. This, for me, is the ultimate win-win. They have a built-in babysitter, I have less financial stress, and I enjoy daily, deeply meaning-ful and often hilarious, interactions with my grandchildren. Memories are being made to last us all for our lifetimes. I know this set-up isn't for everyone, and even fewer would define me as successful based on my income and life circumstances, but for me it is more than enough.

TAKE A DEEPER DIVE

Who is the most successful person you know?
What, in your opinion, makes them successful?

You don't have to limit your answer to one person. For each person you list, share what you personally learned from their trajectory. And remember, a successful person is not necessarily a person with financial wealth.

What life decisions would you have made
differently if money was of no consequence?

Throughout my life I have often fantasized about what I would do if money were no object. Have you? How has your answer changed over your lifetime?

Aside from material possessions, in your
opinion, what does money buy?

Personalize this answer as best you can. What has money (any amount) meant to you and your family? Write about a time where it turned out that money was not the problem solver you thought it would be.

CHAPTER 21

How Much Is Enough:

T I M E

I t's impossible for me to explore the concept of *enough* without addressing time. If all goes well, and I fully expect that it will, I still have more than enough time to deepen my relationships with my family. I will have enough time to travel to new adventurous destinations, make new friends, fall in love, embarrass my children, and work on new creative pursuits.

I have absolutely no idea why I had such a ridiculous sense of urgency to blow through each chapter of my early life, from convincing my parents to let me enroll in kindergarten at just four years old, to graduating high school at sixteen and heading right to college—which I completed at twenty—just in time to get married that same year. My God, what was the rush? Why was I so impatient to move to my next chapter of life when I'd barely taken enough time to relish the current one?

Patience is a powerful use of time. It's a virtue, and one of the most profound examples of compassionate, meditative time management. One of my ever-present, often challenging life goals is to muster up enough patience in all aspects of my life, especially with myself. The challenge of exercising patience through trying times can feel overwhelming, but I am trying. I am really trying to give myself enough time to stop, assess, breathe, and listen.

> Do you consider yourself a patient enough person in all aspects of your life? If not, what tests your patience most?

Taking the time to listen—*really* listen—and not prepare my response while the other person is still talking is time very well spent. It gives me enough of a pause to stave off a snarky or defensive retort. It is a reminder to be more compassionate. This is especially important when negotiating with my five-year-old granddaughter Natalie, equal parts adorable and oppositional. Hearing, "NO! I don't want to stop playing and sit down for dinner" as our freshly plated mac and cheese cools into bowls of congealed orange muck is an opportunity to patiently explain that the food will taste better if it's hot, thus helping Natalie transition to a new activity *and* feel heard. I work on my patience because relishing time with my family is my priority, my spiritual practice, and a chance for deeper personal growth.

More time with my granddaughters is why I uprooted my entire life and moved across the country from California to New York. I feel the deepest sense of love and acceptance when I am with them. Through a five-year-old's eyes, I am enough. When I spend time with Natalie, giving her my full attention, the payoff is enormous. She is my time teacher. I don't rush with her. Time is too precious. When we walk home from school together, I match her pace, try to stay in the moment, and see what she sees. Our three-block walk often takes an hour. Everything catches her attention, from a glittery piece of trash to the bulbous, black-speckled mushroom growing on our neighbor's tree trunk. She must conduct her daily check to see if Lily, the fluffy white pup who lives in the corner house, is taking a nap indoors or *al fresco*. Natalie misses nothing. From her diminutive vantage point, she sees eye to eye with neighborhood canines, giving her a connection with them that deepens my own empathy for animals. "They are just like us," she observes.

There is never enough time to answer all Natalie's questions. She is a geyser of inquisitions and observations, often adding a spritz of non sequiturs that keeps me on my toes. When my kids were young, I figured if they were mature enough to ask a question, they deserved a simple, direct, and honest answer. I do the same with Natalie. When she asked me, "Why is your home so small?" I smiled and explain to her how lucky I am to have my home. My apartment, located just two flights of stairs below hers in the same brownstone, gives me easy access to be with her and her family. I tell her that having my small home so close to hers give us more time together and provides more than enough space for me.

Her question takes me back in time to the large family homes where I raised her mother and her uncle, Sam. Ours was the home where family gatherings, holiday dinners, spontaneous swim parties, and raucous sleepovers took place. Our annual holiday party, which we called Yidfest, was scheduled during Chanukah, and often other families would bring their own menorahs, and our home would be lit with dozens of tiny, twisted colored candles. As we all sang the prayers together in the twinkly glow, time stood still. I gazed at everyone's candle-lit faces, from the youngest children to the oldest *alta cockers*, and thought, *Remember this moment in time. This is more than enough.*

I can always find enough time for Natalie's inquisitions because I know firsthand how time flies. Often when I look at Jenna, her thirty-six-year-old mother, my own daughter, I see Natalie. And vice versa. When I watch Natalie play with the dollhouse my dad built for Jenna thirty years ago, I can relive Jenna's five-year-old delight in endlessly rearranging the furniture in this very same dollhouse. When Natalie plays with all the tiny food in the dollhouse kitchen and admires the platter of cinnamon rolls, the chocolate chip cookies, and the triple layer cake, I am transported to the late 1980s, when her mom and I painstakingly carved them from multiple hues of Fimo clay using manicure scissors, dental floss, and tweezers. I had no idea back then that these thumbnail-size baked goods would stand the test of time, spanning two generations of dollhouse party planning. I watch Natalie's total immersion in the dolls' miniature world, humming a lullaby as she tucks them into their beds, and I am transported to my own domestic fantasy life in

Can you recall a moment in your life that overwhelmed you with a sense of gratitude?

my cardboard box dollhouse when I was her age. I now realize the time I spent furnishing my dollhouse was enough to spark my budding interest in interior design. Decorating my beautiful new Brooklyn apartment began in that ramshackle dollhouse.

At no time in my life did I imagine I would live in New York City. Until 2021, I always thought I would live out my days in California, but here I am, surprised and delighted to be calling Brooklyn home. New York is a cacophony of eccentric people, towering architecture, and an array of aromas, that of a piping hot pepperoni pizza being my favorite.

Can you identify a moment in time that inspired your professional or personal pursuits?

* * *

The discordant blare of honking horns is the soundtrack for New York City. To my ear, honking always sounds like shouting, an audible act of aggression. Honking says, *MOVE! I don't have enough time to wait two to three seconds for you to recognize that the light has changed, so I am going to startle you and your passengers with my honk. I am more alert, present, and mentally sharp than you, and clearly my time is more valuable than yours. Plus, I am having a very bad day!*

Honking is the ultimate act of passive aggression. I want to emphasize *passive* because, let's face it, you are honking while sitting belted in your seat with your window rolled up and your door locked. The only way you could be more passively aggressive would be if you were honking while sleeping.

The only time I think it's okay to honk your horn is if there is imminent danger. You also have my permission to honk if you are an Uber, Lyft, or cab driver transporting an extremely pregnant woman in the final stages of labor because who wants to have a baby in a car? No one, including my mother, who actually gave birth to her fourth child—my baby brother—in the back seat of our family's silver Chevy in the parking lot of Chicago's Michael Reese Hospital. My dad was driving like a harried Mario Andretti down Lake Shore Drive from Skokie, a North suburb, to the South Side, where the hospital was located. The doctor met them in the ER parking lot, delivered my brother, whisked him and my mother into the hospital, shot my dad a sympathetic smile, and said, "Thank heavens for your plastic seat covers."

* * *

How do you measure time? By birthdays? The calendar year? Or . . . ?

"How do you measure a year in a life?" wrote Jonathan Larson, composer of the hit Broadway musical, *Rent.* That song, "Seasons of Love," gave us the earworm, "Five hundred twenty-five thousand, six hundred minutes," the number of minutes in a year. Tragically, Larson didn't live to see *Rent* open on Broadway, a heartbreaking example of why we should never assume that we have enough time left to do the things we want to do. How precious and unpredictable our time together can be.

I try not to waste my time or that of others. I am a punctual person. Early in my middle-life dating adventures, I connected with a man online, and for our first date we agreed to meet at a trendy coffee shop at five p.m. When I arrived, the guy brusquely announced that I was late.

What must you do in order to feel you haven't wasted the day? Do you consider relaxation wasteful, or can it be purposeful?

I glanced down at my watch, which read exactly five p.m., then looked up again with a confused expression. "It's five on the dot. I'm not late."

He tersely responded, "Early is on time. Now you are late."

What a prickly first impression, and no, there wasn't a second date.

My close circle of friends and family can attest that I am rarely late for anything, including a date, a dinner reservation, a party, or a Zoom meeting. Being on time is a commitment to my coworkers, friends, loved ones, and prospective romantic partners that I value their time as much as my own. Procrastinators seem to have their own sense of time. This can be confounding for decisive people like me who take satisfaction in not putting anything off or leaving anything unsaid. I was supremely tested when I dated a master procrastinator who was charming and kind, but lived in a perpetual state of denial and procrastinated about most aspects of his life. We stopped seeing each other; I think I left him a message or two, but he didn't call back, and that was that. A year later, we had a friendly chance meeting on a street in my neighborhood, and I realized he had actually procrastinated about breaking up with me until I would just assume we were no longer dating.

* * *

My dad always loved to play Scrabble, even at ninety-two years old, when his sense of time and place was lost to dementia and his short-term memory was gone. Many of my fondest memories of his final years are of watching him deep in concentration, hunched over his mid-century Scrabble board, scrutinizing his tiles and laying down the most outrageous words. I never corrected him, dutifully kept score, and did my best to connect something

Are you able to make enough time for people who are important to you?

to his cockamamie wordsmithing. His invented two-letter words were legendary. He would put down a word like *KS*, then stare at me with a sparkle in his eyes, waiting for me to challenge him. "*KS* is a word," he'd argue. "It's a teeny kiss." He'd smile devilishly at me just like he smiled at my mom over the forty-plus years they played Scrabble together. My mom would chide him for cheating, and he would just smile that smile and she'd never challenge him to look up his goofy words in the dictionary. Their time playing Scrabble was enough to keep them happily connected, celebrating each other's triumphant seven-letter-word throwdowns, even through tough times.

Toward the end of my father's life, dementia left him stumped by Scrabble and turned most conversations into repetitive spirals. I looked forward to our visits nonetheless. Even if we just sat on the porch together and watched the cars drive by, singing along to a Frank Sinatra song blasting from his iPod, our time spent together was precious and always time well spent.

What's your most vivid example of the passing of time?

Watching my mom and dad age was an agonizing way to mark time. Along with my dad's dementia, there were chronic health challenges and my mom's mental illness that affected their quality of life. I am grateful I really did have enough time with both of my parents in the final chapters of their lives. We lived close to each other, which made all the difference. I have no regrets, no woulda-coulda-shouldas. I hope my children will feel the same way at the end of my life. I hope we will have had enough quality time together to make memories that will endure long after I'm gone.

* * *

Does a busy schedule filled with work appointments and social events equal a good, fulfilling life? Or can your life be big enough, meaningful enough, and productive enough without every hour spoken for? Do you have friends or family members who thrive on chaos and perpetually complain that they never have enough time for self-care? Some people fill their days with meetings, appointments, caregiving, and social obligations choreographed with incessant hand-wringing over things they have no control over. If they took all the time they spent complaining about not having enough time, they'd have enough time for an around-the-world cruise.

My adult son, Sam, is serious about his twice-daily meditation practice and schedules his twenty-minute sessions with the same sense of purpose as his most important business meetings. Coworkers have commented on his impressive time management skills and self-care commitment. Other partners in his start-up, inspired by his discipline, have also scheduled meditation sessions, and the consensus is that their corporate culture benefits.

If you were able to travel back in time, where would you go and when would it be?

I must admit that I don't have my son's discipline. I haven't dedicated enough time or effort to a regular practice of self-care. I am in a chapter of my life where I embrace free time, less structure, fewer social obligations, and spontaneous fun. When I lived in Los Angeles, my calendar was often filled with invitations, professional commitments, and stressful deadlines. In my Brooklyn life, I just exhale and remind myself it is enough to simply enjoy my free time.

* * *

I think some parents overschedule their children's time. Taking Jaydon to soccer followed by art class every Monday, trumpet Tuesdays and Thursdays, and swimming lessons on Fridays may give him multifaceted opportunities to discover his true gifts, but come on, he's only five. Why not wait until six to start the trumpet? I know, some kids really do thrive on being busy. I wonder, though, in this age of highly structured school days, if kids get enough time to just be kids, letting their imaginations take them on their own adventures.

The Beauty of Boredom

Do you consider boredom time wasted, or time for relaxation? When was the last time you let yourself get bored enough to daydream? I like to think of boredom as a mindful meditation, a chance to refresh and recharge. Here are a few benefits of boredom:

1. Boredom is an opportunity to explore your creative side. Focus on a single color and let it take your mind on a journey. Will the color blue take you to the ocean, the sky, the color of your lover's eyes?
2. Boredom is a chance to reconnect with nature. Venture out to your local park with no clear intention or destination. Breathe deeply, notice the colors of the leaves, the softness of the soil beneath your feet. Take enough time to feel connected to the natural elements around you before heading indoors.

3. Boredom is an inside job. With no plan to accomplish anything, roam the rooms of your home. Peer into drawers or closets you haven't investigated for a while. Stare deep into family photos and remember what you were doing, thinking, and feeling when the picture was taken. Resist the instinct to clean or organize. Just observe and reclaim something new about your home, its contents, and, ultimately, yourself.

I am a huge believer in the beauty of boredom. When my kids were young and complained that they were bored, I often accused them of not having enough of an imagination. That usually woke them up to all they had available to entertain themselves. After the predictably timed eye roll, Sam usually gravitated toward something musical and Jenna often picked up a book or got lost in her virtual Sims world.

I believe passions developed out of my childhood boredom. Experimenting in the kitchen as a preteen was the start of my love for all things culinary. Pressing my ear against the family HiFi stereo listening to comedy albums over and over and over again introduced me to the concept of comedy as a viable career. These days, I've added Internet shopping, social media scrolling, and binge watching *The Bear* on Hulu as rewards for accomplishing something significant. Who says bribery can't be an effective time management tool?

What are your favorite time management tools?

I love making lists. I get an inordinate amount of satisfaction crossing tasks off lists. For me, a fully crossed-off list, whether it is handwritten or on my iPhone note pad, is enough proof that I am accomplished, successful, and productive, even if it's just a grocery list. Bravo to me for not forgetting pickles. Or chocolate.

One of the reasons I love cooking so much is that it exists in its own time frame. You cannot will water to boil. You cannot summon bread dough to rise before it is ready. You cannot rush a simmer. Cooking is time-sensitive, a constant reminder that we cannot control time. When I take enough time to organize and prep for a multicourse meal, I feel like a culinary orchestral conductor, utterly absorbed in the delicate syncopation of getting everything cooked and on the table at the right temperature at the same time.

Brownies are my favorite culinary example of the magical power of time. They never seem quite done when you take them out of the oven at the prescribed time, but you must trust that they have cooked enough. If you follow directions, you will be richly rewarded with a firm, lightly-cracked top and a dense, gooey center. Is there anything better than biting into a warm brownie? Well, maybe two, because one is rarely enough.

Since there are more than enough premade foods at the market and food delivery is so easy, do you consider cooking from scratch a waste of time?

I have worked jobs both at night and during the day. The list is surprisingly diverse, including stand-up comic and preschool cooking instructor. These jobs required very different levels of adrenaline and time management, never affording me the luxury to contemplate my circadian rhythm.

So, whether you are on a deadline, have time on your hands, are experiencing a pregnant pause, getting time and a half, finding time, wasting time, on overtime, moving double time, on borrowed time, or doing time, please remember to live in the moment. May every minute you have left be filled with at least one precious second of bliss, and may it be enough.

TAKE A DEEPER DIVE

Think about how you schedule time with your family.
List your favorite shared rituals and routines.

List ways you would like to restructure your family time. Would your family members welcome these ideas? If not, how do you think your family would like to spend time together?

Now think about how you schedule time for yourself.
List your favorite solo rituals and activities.

Are you content with your work/family/self balance? Imagine you had two hours every day that were 100 percent yours to do whatever you like. How would you spend it?

The late Rose Fitzgerald Kennedy was quoted
as saying, "It has been said that time heals all
wounds. I don't agree." What do you think?

If you agree, share an example of when time proved to have healing powers, If you agree with Rose Kennedy that time does not heal all wounds, explain why you've come to that conclusion.

CHAPTER 22

How Much Is Enough:

LIFE

Are there any life chapters you would change if you could? When I reflect back on mine, I vividly remember many challenging ones: my parents' deaths, my son Sam's illness, the end of my thirty-year marriage, beginning my solo life at fifty, and, most recently, leaving everything familiar and safe in sunny California to start my life anew across the country in Brooklyn, New York, at sixty-four. Strange as it sounds, I am filled with gratitude for every one of those difficult life passages. With the perspective only a sixty-plus-year-old possesses, I now know that those experiences strengthened my spine, honed my sense of humor, redefined my sense of self, and deepened my definition of family. All of these challenges were enough to prove true John Lennon's sage advice, "Everything will be okay in the end. If it's not okay, it's not the end."

My life has also given me more than enough personal insight into the struggle with mental illness. My mother spent most of her life struggling with manic and depressive episodes that had a profound impact on every aspect of her life, especially her parenting. As I wrote this book, I often found myself pondering her inner life. Did she lament unrequited loves, unfulfilled career trajectories, unrealized dreams of solo travel? Did she often fantasize about a life different than her own? We were a relentless crew, never

Do you feel as if you have truly lived enough of your life on your own terms?

giving her enough space or time to contemplate any other life path. She was a teacher before she had children, and I'm sure the patience learned from managing classrooms full of unruly kids came in handy as we got older and grew more demanding. We wore her down. I knew it for sure once I had kids and experienced my own moments of mind-numbing exhaustion. To capture enough time for myself in the maelstrom of motherhood was an elusive wish that was simply out of reach.

My life involved ping-ponging among eleven homes scattered across two states—Illinois and California—before I turned twenty-one. Throughout my childhood, my father's work with Motorola transferred our family cross country and back again, often smack in the middle of a school year, rarely giving me enough time to form meaningful, lasting friendships. Looking back, I now realize that moving around that much also had an upside. It gave me more than enough opportunities to establish a deeper sense of independence and opportunities for reinvention that accompanied each move.

Every time I settled into a new school, I observed the deep roots my classmates shared, silently bemoaning the fact that I would never have enough time to build ties laced with that sort of rich, shared history. I did my best to fit into social cliques that had been formed in preschool with kids who basically grew up together sharing clothes, countless birthday sleepovers, and their virginity at prom afterparties.

New kids were rare at all of my new schools, so my siblings and I were often perceived as interlopers appearing from other parts unknown. This was our mountain to climb, a solo trek, independent from our parents, who had their own challenges: my mom, overwhelmed by having to set up a completely new home every few years and enroll four kids in new schools; and my dad, always focused on ingratiating himself to his coworkers with each newly elevated role within Motorola.

When I moved as a high school freshman from Los Angeles to a Chicago suburb, my classmates assumed I had gone to school with movie stars. Few had ever been to California, so television and movies informed their La La Land impressions. I was slow to correct them, as it gave me an interesting if undeserved and somewhat dishonest backstory. I was willing to fudge the truth if it got me invited to the right parties with the cool kids, who were too busy being popular to fact-check. Had I lived near the Brady Bunch? Hung out with the Partridge Family? Rubbed shoulders with the Monkees? Well, my home was located in the same valley (San Fernando) as the Bradys, I once saw David Cassidy shopping at my local mall, and I saw the Monkees perform at the Hollywood Bowl. Does that count?

At sixty-six, I am still searching for opportunities to hang with those cool kids from my youth. Most of them are now married, in their sixties, retired, or living thousands of miles away from me. Every moment with them is precious. Time together must often be scheduled months in advance. Once we see each other, there never seems to be enough time to get caught up before one or the other of us heads home.

I watch my close friends age and marvel at how their faces, bodies, and, most importantly, their spirits remain familiar and ageless to me. I am amazed that, despite my transient life, I've stayed closely connected to friends from high school, college, and the early days of my career. We've known each other for over forty years, but in a strange way our friendships remain unchanged from our early days. Life whirls around us, braiding the birth of children and grandchildren, the deaths of parents, new homes, and career trajectories in and out of our lives as proof that time has passed. For me, our friendships possess enough magic to stop time.

Whose life do you admire most and why?

Regardless of my health regime, spiritual practice, or trendy hair style, I am aware that I cannot stop aging. There will never be enough exercises, anti-aging serums, plastic surgeries, sex drive supplements, or hormone replacements to turn back the clock. No amount of wealth or professional accomplishments can stop time. I have friends who cannot accept that they are over sixty years old, and even though their bodies, fashion aesthetic, and taste in music seems incongruous with their chronology, the truth is that for them, and for all of us, the days in our lives are numbered. I don't say this to be maudlin. Being in acceptance can be enough of a reason for me to celebrate every new day with gratitude that I, and my loved ones, have arrived at the here and now.

Remember Me

Give your loved ones enough information to keep your memory alive for generations to come. The questions you've answered throughout this book can become a valuable historical document. In addition to these questions, consider registering for questions to ponder on https://doyou10q.com/. Once a year, in the fall, DoYou10Q will email you ten questions in ten days and then secure your answers in a secret online vault, to be sent back to you via email one year later for you to chronicle and contemplate. I love their slogan: *10Q: Reflect. React. Renew. Life's Biggest Questions. Answered By You.*

Reflecting back on my career, one of my many highlights was working for HGTV, hosting a series called *Fantasy Open House*, where we toured extravagant, high-end residences for sale. This combined several of my passions—interior design, travel, comedy, and meeting new people. I was hired because the network wanted a host who would never actually live in these houses but say all the things the viewers were thinking. My improv training came in handy. I was fortunate to work with Cheri Peters, a talented, insightful showrunner who had previously produced *The Lifestyles of the Rich and Famous.* Thanks to Robin Leach, she knew the importance of a comedic, irreverent host.

I was more than happy to do all the promotional work associated with my HGTV hosting duties. I was even able to take part in a huge, life-changing moment for Kathy Hedrick, a Kansas City school teacher who was the 2001 "HGTV Dream Home Giveaway" winner. The network arranged to have me pop into her classroom unannounced as she taught her students, proclaiming that she was the official "HGTV Dream Home Giveaway" winner. When I awarded Kathy a magnificent home in Penobscot Bay, Maine, along with a brand new car, I was overwhelmed with excitement that I'd had a role in changing this beloved educator's life forever.

The HGTV camera crew captured everything. She was stunned, speechless, and teary trying to comprehend what just happened, as her students bolted from their desks, rushing to the front of the classroom to congratulate her. Once she caught her breath, Kathy shared that she was a single parent with a teenage son who was just learning how to drive. The new car would have been more than enough of a life-changing prize, as her current vehicle was often towed in and out of her mechanic's garage. The new home was inconceivable, as she had never in her wildest fantasies imagined owning a home as grand as this. She had entered the contest because HGTV was her favorite network. She watched HGTV all the time but never, ever expected that she would be the one to win their annual Dream Home Giveaway.

Life is so full of surprises for all of us. Just when you've settled into a life where you believe you have enough, something happens and your concept of enough gets turned upside down.

One of the luxurious homes we shot for *Fantasy Open House* was owned by Gene, a soft-spoken man with terminal brain cancer and, surprisingly, one of the most upbeat, positive people I've ever met. The gnarly scar that circled the top of his bald scalp—imagine a punk rocker's yarmulke—was his defiant fashion statement. He exuded a sense of triumphant, unexpected contentment. We had plenty of time to chat as our production crew spent over nine hours shooting every richly appointed niche of his beautiful Rancho Santa Fe, California estate for a fifteen-minute segment on an upcoming episode of our show. Something he told me that day has always stayed with me. He said, "You know the best thing about terminal cancer? No more bad days. I wake up. It's a great day."

I've lost track of how many times I have thought of this dear man and his effervescent approach to the end of his life. His words come to me when I am stressing over something insignificant. *Snap out of it, Claire. It is enough just to wake up healthy.*

A quick Google search on "genome sequencing" tells us that only 4 percent of our mortality is genetic. So as I career on the precarious path toward my golden years, I realize I must accept responsibility for 96 percent of my life. I am aware that years of happily scarfing down bags of potato chips, fried chicken, and See's dark chocolate Bordeaux bars may contribute to my expiration date, but I refuse to live my life with regrets.

* * *

As you face the end of your life, do you think you'll have the courage to say, "Enough is enough"? My parents lived in Leisure World in Seal Beach, California, where poolside discussions of end-of-life plans were as common as critiquing last night's Early Bird Meatloaf Special. Most of my parents' neighbors were in their eighties and nineties, so conversations about the terms of their individual DNRs (Do Not Resuscitate) were much more practical than maudlin.

On one of many visits to Leisure World, or, as my dad affectionately called it, "Seizure World," I went to the community library with my dad. He walked me over to the Hemlock Society section, located in a sunny corner. He pulled out several books on assisted suicide and calmly shared his wishes with me. He went on to explain that he had changed his end of life wishes legally and that he expected me to help him should the time come when he could no longer be independent and take care of himself. It didn't occur to me to argue with him. It was clear he had thought this through, and I prayed we'd have more than enough time together before this subject would be revisited. I was relieved that he had considered these matters while he was still coherent enough to make his own arrangements, so I and my siblings wouldn't have to. Little did I know, within a year after this conversation, dementia would ruthlessly rob him of his memory.

As promised, I helped my father end his life in his ninety-third year. The week that he died began when he slipped in the shower and broke his hip. His short-term memory was gone, so by the time the ambulance arrived, less than five minutes after his fall, he had no idea why they were there or why he couldn't move his leg. My son and I sat across from each other as my dad laid between us on the ER gurney, asking every few minutes when we could go out to eat. We gently repeated that he had broken his hip and would be admitted to the hospital for surgery. It turned into a perverse version of *Groundhog Day*, with him asking us the very same question moments after we had answered.

As he was wheeled into surgery, I gave him a tight hug and said good-bye with the expectation that I might not see him alive again. Miraculously, he survived his surgery. My dad came out of the anesthesia with his hip reattached, but mentally he was even more discombobulated, confused, and upset than before. He uncharacteristically yelled at the nurses to get him out of bed and refused any form of physical therapy. "Why do I need it? I'm fine. Hand me my pants. Let's just go home!"

The doctors told me the combination of his dementia, his age, and

> **Has your life turned out as you imagined it would be? What was the biggest surprise?**

his unwillingness to do any sort of PT would keep him bed bound for the remainder of his life. I told his doctor that was against his end-of-life plan, and we agreed on hospice care. I was instructed by his doctors the correct way to ask the hospice nurse for the legal limit of morphine to honor my dad's request. He stopped eating, and we forced nothing on him or in him. Within days, his body began shutting down. He began having touching conversations with my mother, gone over ten years, before sliding into a gentle morphine coma. I was touched to witness my parents' reconnection before he passed away.

Both my parents were always clear with my siblings and me about not wanting funerals or burials. They signed all the paperwork and donated their bodies to the University of California medical schools. We learned of their wishes at an early age. Growing up, we often heard, "If you need a stone in the ground to remember us after we're gone, we clearly didn't have enough fun together when we were alive."

Have you left anything unsaid to your loved ones with the assumption that you have enough time to do so?

Upon my dad's death, the medical school van arrived to pick up his body. As I watched the van drive away, I prayed some students would find something miraculous from studying his corpse. Maybe that a burn victim would receive some of my dad's thick skin. I hoped someone new would see life through his inquisitive eyes. Perhaps his beautiful heart brought someone else solace, the way it comforted me. I was at peace with his departure. He had lived a good life and he had enough. It was exactly what he asked for that day in the Leisure World library.

* * *

For those in recovery from addiction, life begins twice: at birth and with sobriety. Throughout the seventeen years I have sat in the rooms of Twelve Step meetings, I remain deeply moved by the life and death struggles that others shared, many of which depict inconceivable suffering and shocking tragedy, for both the addict and their loved ones. I am reminded how precious life is every time I hear one of these shares. And I consider how fragile and impermanent my healthy life is, a life I take for granted because I was not raised by addicts or alcoholics and didn't suffer through the anger, abuse, and neglect that accompanied too many people's childhoods.

I think about my own children and consider how living with an addict-alcoholic father has affected their lives. I watch and wonder if my love is enough to compensate for the tumult. Was my devotion enough to fill the void substance abuse inevitably brings into a family? Was my decision to end the marriage enough of a warning to my kids that addiction has no place in a happy marriage?

They are now grown. Their lives, their careers, and their relationships, along with every daily decision, are theirs to make. With a huge sigh of relief, I can report, so far, so good. I remain an eager, loving bystander and cheerleader. I may have given them life, but the life I must focus on now is my own, such a strange counterintuitive act for a steadfast parent like me. I've done enough foundational parenting. I fed, clothed, educated, and deeply cared for them as they grew. Now my daughter has children of her own to tend to and I have this new chapter of my life to contemplate. I now step back, with deep respect for the adults my children have become and the lives they lead. It is miraculous, and it is enough.

TAKE A DEEPER DIVE

Do you have any nagging regrets?

Write them down and rank them in order of possibility for resolution. If there is still a chance to make a change, an amend, or a travel itinerary, write out a plan of attack for each to shorten your list of regrets.

How do you define "acting your age"?

I have no idea what 'acting my age' means. Please share your thoughts on this phrase, both as it applies to you and in comparison to your parents.

If you had the opportunity to live your life over again, would you do anything differently?

Take time to contemplate this very personal question and answer as honestly as you can. The answer to this question can be a huge gift from you to you. Think of it as a future mission statement, understanding that there is still time in your life to make important changes. If you have children, consider sharing this answer with them to open up lines of communication that could create renewed closeness and a deeper understanding.

CHAPTER 23

How Much Is Enough:

YOUR "ENOUGH" INVENTORY

Here are all the questions from the chapters in one convenient list. Together, your answers will form a record of your thoughts about the meaning of *enough* in twenty-two aspects of life. Your "Enough" Inventory could be a record you'd like to hand down to future generations, or it could be something you reflect upon privately. Either way, I hope you'll find it useful.

Continue the conversation with me and other readers on Facebook! https://facebook.com/howmuchisenoughbook

Chapter 1: Space

1. How does your mindset change when you change spaces?
2. If money were no object, how many homes would be enough for you?
3. How do you define your sense of self through your space? Reflect on all the places you've lived, noting your age, financial status, and what you loved about each place.
4. How have your life circumstances changed your living space requirements?
5. If you've only lived in small spaces, do you think living in a larger space would feel decadent or discombobulating?
6. What treasured possessions or small items could you place in your home to invoke comforting memories or fulfill wishes?
7. Do you have a storage space? What items are you storing? What items are you hiding?

8. Describe your dream space by drawing it, writing about it, or creating a Pinterest vision board.

Chapter 2: Apparel

1. What was the first article of clothing that gave you enough confidence to embrace your individuality?
2. When did you first define your identity through apparel?
3. At what age did comfort matter more than style?
4. How often do you admire a pair of shoes or an article of clothing, look at the price tag, and think, Will I wear this enough to justify the price?
5. What percentage of your daily outfits are chosen to impress others?
6. Do you own pair of shoes or an article of clothing that can be enough to alter your mood or identity the minute you put them on?
7. What is your earliest memory of a well-dressed person? Does this memory still inform your own apparel choices, or has your sense of style changed?
8. What is enough of a reason to buy a new clothing item: Style? Comfort? Status? Revenge?
9. How old were you when you first looked in the mirror and believed you were attractive enough?
10. What's your definition of dressing for success?
11. Do you feel the way your kids dress(ed) is a reflection of your parenting?
12. What new chapter of life inspired you enough to change your personal style?
13. How do you define "dressing your age"?
14. Look into your closet and say out loud, "I have enough clothes, enough shoes, enough accessories." What emotions surface when you make this proclamation? Is this a true statement? How much of your wardrobe do you actually wear?
15. Imagine you had to narrow your wardrobe down to six items of clothing. Which items would they be?

16. Do you own garments or accessories that have equal parts sentimental value and functionality? List each such item along with a story illustrating its sentimental value. Share an example of an occasion where you are most comfortable wearing the item.
17. Complete this sentence: If money were no object, I would wear . . .

Chapter 3: Exercise

1. What do you consider your strongest physical ability?
2. What do you currently do for exercise? How has your exercise regime changed over the years?
3. Do you know your target heart rate? Do you know how to build muscle? (See the sidebar in chapter 3!)
4. What activities do you enjoy that really are exercise even though you don't think of them as such?
5. Do you consider walking enough of a workout?
6. What nonprofessional person do you admire for their physical acumen? Do you aspire to be like them?
7. Imagine you could win an Olympic medal in any sport, real or imagined. What would the sport be, and why has it captured your imagination?
8. What physical accomplishment are you most proud of?

Chapter 4: Childhood

1. At what age did you decide whether to start a family? Are you at peace today with your decision?
2. In your opinion, did your parents have enough children? Too many? Too few?
3. Was there a point in your childhood when you didn't feel you had enough? How did you manage that feeling?
4. If you could pick anyone in the world to be your parents (not

counting your own), who would you pick and why?

5. What do you remember most vividly about your childhood that you have carried into your role as a parent?

6. If you are a parent, would you say you had enough children, or would you have liked to have more?

7. How do you feel parenthood or the decision not to have children defines your day-to-day decisions?

8. What does a good enough parent look like? Did your parents give you enough attention? Support? Food, clothing, safety? Encouragement for your educational and personal pursuits?

9. Do you feel you had enough fun with your children? Looking back, what would you do differently?

10. What was the best piece of advice your parents gave you? How have you applied it in your life? What advice have you given your own children that resonated enough with them to change their behavior?

11. What advice would you give your fifteen-year-old self, knowing what you know today?

Chapter 5: Family

1. As a child, did you long for kin different than your own, or did you receive more than enough love and support from your family of origin?

2. How often have you thought (or said) "Enough!" during a family conversation?

3. How did your grandparents influence your parents' parenting of you?

4. Where might one find a family of choice? (My ideas are in the sidebar in chapter 5.)

5. Have you had enough of a family member's behavior and consciously ended your relationship with them?

6. What are the most impactful lessons you learned from your family?

7. What role did you play in your family dynamic?

8. Do you believe you chose your parents?

9. What aspect of your personality do you attribute to your family?

10. Did you ever wish you had someone else's parents? How old were you and what were the circumstances? Whose parents did you covet? What made them so attractive? How has your concept of the ideal parent changed with age? If you are now a parent, which of your ideal parents' attributes did you include in your parenting arsenal?

11. What family traits would you like to be passed down to the next generation?

12. Would you be friends with your sibling(s) today if you weren't related by blood? Take a moment to think about each of your siblings. List qualities of theirs you admire. Also list qualities that pose a challenge. Are these qualities enough to forge a lifelong friendship as adults?

Chapter 6: Health

1. Reflecting back to the year 2020, would you say you took enough health precautions?

2. How many of your health challenges do you attribute to family genetics?

3. Are you and your loved ones current on all vaccinations?

4. Have you considered making a DNR (a "do not resuscitate" order)?

5. How are you feeling today? Are you healthy enough to enjoy the day?

6. What is your personal definition of "good enough" health?

7. Has your parents' health—good or bad—been enough of an inspiration to impact your self-care?

8. What are you most proud of about your health? List the top five health assets you possess and how they enhance your life. Expand this list with ways you commit to good health.

9. How many of your health challenges do you attribute to family genetics?

10. Has your child's health ever taken a toll on your mental health? How did you move through it?

Chapter 7: Marriage

1. Did your parents' marriage give you enough positive or negative reasons to ponder the merits of marriage?
2. What role—if any—did drugs and alcohol play in your courtship? Would you say they were enough of a social lubricant to alter your perception of romance?
3. Can you think of an apology that could be improved by replacing 'but' with 'and'?
4. Do you believe that marriage is a spiritual bond?
5. What tricks could partners use to avoid going to bed angry? (See my ideas in the last sidebar in chapter 7.)
6. What do you think is a good enough reason to end a marriage?
7. Can an open marriage be enough of a marriage commitment for you?
8. Do you think the concept of marriage is outdated? If yes, what aspects of marriage do you think are outdated? If your answer is no, elaborate on the aspects of marriage that make sense in your life. Share your valuable opinion of marriage in your personal journal or with your trusted tribe.
9. If you chose to end a marriage, when did you know you'd had enough?
10. Do you know many happy, single people? If you are a happy, single person, what's the secret to your happiness?

Chapter 8: Friendship

1. What did you learn from your childhood friendships?
2. How do your friendships affect your day-to-day decision-making?
3. What was the most unexpected place you found a close friend?
4. Do you have close platonic friends of the opposite sex?
5. What are your reasons for ending a friendship?
6. What are some ways you could make new friends? (My suggestions are in the sidebar in chapter 8.)

7. Are you more inclined to reach out to friends when good things happen or when bad things happen?

8. Who is your oldest friend and what is your secret to maintaining that friendship?

9. At what points in your life did you form your closest friendship(s)? How do you define a close friend? Is it history? Shared interests? Serendipity? Reflect on the times in your life you met someone and just knew they'd be your friend for life. List life passages where friendships seemed to develop organically.

10. Do your friendships enhance or challenge your relationship with your primary partner? Do you have mutual friends? Is there jealousy? Write about the role your friendships play in your relationship.

Chapter 9: Food

1. Is there a meal that holds an indelible memory for you?

2. What's your comfort food that you can never get enough of?

3. What's the menu and location of your fantasy meal?

4. Have you tried fufu? (Find this and other ideas for experiencing new cuisines in the first sidebar in chapter 9.)

5. As a parent, did you worry that your kids didn't eat enough?

6. How do you know when you've eaten enough? Is satiety more physical or emotional for you?

7. Have you ever tried container gardening? Share a picture of your container garden—no matter how small—in my Facebook group at https://facebook.com/howmuchisenoughbook.

8. Were your school lunches sustenance enough to get you through the school day?

9. Do you have a happy childhood memory that involves food?

10. Do you consider yourself a passionate eater? A restrictive eater?

11. Do you struggle with the concept of enough when it comes to food?

12. Do you eat for pleasure, for fuel, or a combination of both? Write about a typical day of eating for you. Are you someone who plans

each meal, or do you eat whatever is fast, easy, and available? If you live with others, does everyone in your home have a similar approach to eating? If no, elaborate on the discord.

13. What role does cuisine play in your vacation planning? Do you have a favorite cuisine? Have you ever planned a gastronomic getaway with this cuisine in mind? List favorite vacation bites, meals, and memories that were as delicious as they were picturesque.

14. Would you say you have a healthy relationship with food? If yes, what or whom do you credit for that healthy relationship? Explain this person's role in and impact on your life.

Chapter 10: Travel

1. Who in your life could use the gift of travel? (I've listed some travel gift ideas in the first sidebar in chapter 10.)

2. What trip have you taken that has stayed with you throughout your entire life? What made it so memorable?

3. Do past road trips contain enough happy memories to make you want to plan another one?

4. What childhood travel memory would you prefer never to revisit?

5. If you had enough money and time to book a dream vacation, what would be your itinerary?

6. Would you travel solo? (If you need encouragement, see the second sidebar in chapter 10.)

7. Do you feel you have traveled enough in your life?

8. What is your favorite mode of transportation?

9. Has a trip ever changed your life? How?

10. Do you think multigenerational trips can be relaxing for all? If yes, how do you accomplish that? Share details of your best multigenerational trip. What advice would you give to someone contemplating a multigenerational vacation?

11. What sort of trip would take you outside your comfort zone? Would you find it enlightening? Detail the trip that has created the most

profound memories. Would you take this trip again?

12. When has travel served as an escape for you? Were you able to find enough solace to return home with a renewed attitude?

Chapter 11: Work

1. Did your education provide enough preparation for your chosen profession?

2. Have you thought about changing careers? (There are support systems for that! See the sidebar in chapter 11.)

3. Do you feel you had enough time with your family as you launched your career? Looking back, what would you have done differently?

4. How has your family influenced your professional career decisions?

5. If you are self-employed, do you have a ritual to signify the end of your workday?

6. How did the pandemic change your work/life balance?

7. Knowing what you know today, what work/life advice would you like to give your younger self?

8. In which chapter of your professional life were you the happiest both personally and professionally?

9. Do you believe your employer offers enough benefits and compensation for the work you deliver? If no, what more would you like to receive?

10. Most of us have worked jobs we consider unrelated to our careers. Looking back on your own working life, is there anything a job taught you that your career did not?

11. Whose work/life balance do you admire? What do they do for work, and how do they strike a balance?

12. What's your dream job? How closely does it resemble your actual job?

Chapter 12: Substances

1. What would you say is your most personally challenging substance?
2. How much was enough alcohol in your childhood home?
3. Do you trust yourself to know how much is enough when it comes to enjoying substances? If yes, has this always been the case?
4. Do you sometimes wear yourself out solving other people's problems? (The sidebar in chapter 12 might help you.)
5. Has your life or the life of someone you love been touched by substance abuse? What have you learned from this experience?
6. Is it the chronic substance use or the deception and dishonesty that accompanies substance abuse that would give you pause to say 'Enough'?
7. What are the pros and cons of substance use in your personal life?

Chapter 13: Fun

1. Is having enough fun part of your daily practice?
2. If you answered 'no' to the above, see the sidebar in chapter 13 for some ways to add more fun to your day. If you have mastered the art of daily fun, please join my Facebook group (https://facebook.com/howmuchisenoughbook) and tell other readers how you do it.
3. What's the most fun you have had parenting?
4. Are you having enough fun at work? If the answer is no, what's holding you back?
5. How has incorporating fun into your life impacted your health?
6. Can you cite an example from your own life where an injection of humor was enough to improve a prickly situation?
7. What role does fun play in your daily life? For one whole day, try keeping a log of each time you find yourself having fun.
8. Do you think one can have too much fun?
9. Do you believe a sense of fun is a conscious choice or an innate instinct? Whom do you consider your go-to friend when you want to

have fun? List the qualities you admire most about this friend and how they bring fun into your life.

Chapter 14: Education

1. Who taught you the most profound lessons in your life?
2. Did you find enough value in your education when you were young?
3. Was a formal education a financial priority in your family? Was there enough money to go to college?
4. Was there someone in your life who gave you a deeper appreciation for your education?
5. When did you know you'd had enough formal education?
6. How do you stay curious about the world? (Find some ideas in the sidebar in chapter 14.)
7. Do you think our current public education system gives enough credence to the different ways boys and girls learn?
8. In what ways do you feel formal education has been instrumental in your personal or professional success?
9. Did anyone ever tell you that you weren't "college material"? Did you believe them?
10. Do you think you learned enough practical life skills at school?
11. Who was your all-time favorite teacher? What made this teacher so impactful? How have their lessons stayed with you through adulthood?
12. Knowing what you know now, what advice would you give your younger self about choosing an academic path?
13. Do you believe you have both an EQ—emotional intelligence—and an IQ—intellectual intelligence?

Chapter 15: Beauty

1. What's the most beautiful place you've ever visited?

2. Look at photos of yourself from each decade of your life. What made you feel beautiful then? Who gave you confidence to feel beautiful? Write yourself a heartfelt compliment for each decade.

3. At what point in your life did you come to understand your own unique brand of beauty?

4. As a child, did you ever feel "less than" because you didn't look a certain way? How did you counteract that feeling?

5. What role does social media play in your definition of beauty?

6. What sort of pain or discomfort are you willing to endure in the name of beauty?

7. Do you have a go-to outfit that makes you feel especially beautiful? Where and when do you wear it? Why does this outfit make you feel special? Did you buy it for yourself or was it a gift?

8. Besides physical appearance, what represents beauty in your life? Make a list. Let your imagination go wild.

9. Who represents your ideal definition of beauty and why? Don't limit your answer to only physical beauty. List at least five people. What qualities do they possess that you would like to emulate?

Chapter 16: Memory

1. What is your earliest memory?

2. What do you want people to remember about you? (See the sidebar in chapter 16 for some ways to preserve memories for future generations.)

3. Does your selective memory help you recall enough happy memories to balance the unhappy ones?

4. Are some memories better left unrecovered?

5. In your most vivid memories, which of your five senses are most often featured?

6. What was playing on the radio the night you got your first kiss? What memories does that song conjure up for you?

7. How do your childhood memories differ from your siblings'

memories? Pick a memorable occasion and see if everyone remembers the same details.

8. How have memories informed your decision-making? List several memories and explain the role each played in your subsequent decisions.

9. Which of your memories do you most want to share with the next generation? Write a letter to your family about them and store it with your will and estate papers.

Chapter 17: Love

1. Do you harbor a secret fantasy about the one that got away?
2. How much love is enough?
3. Would you say the presence of an animal created more love in your life? If yes, in what way?
4. What is your love language: Words of Affirmation, Quality Time, Gifts, Acts of Service, or Physical Touch?
5. Do you believe there is only one great love in each of our lives?
6. What's the most memorable example of love you've ever witnessed? Think beyond romantic love. Can you list ten examples?
7. Who has made you feel most loved in your life? Write a letter to them, whether they are dead or alive, and detail all the ways their love has brought you growth, joy, and serenity.
8. Do you believe in love at first sight? Have you experienced it? Think about love in the broadest sense before you answer.

Chapter 18: Sex

1. How much is enough sex for you to feel positively connected to your body?
2. How has your attitude about sex changed as you've gotten older?
3. If you are a parent, do you feel you did a good enough job teaching

your children about sex? Did your parents give you enough information regarding your sex education?

4. Have you ever felt shame for using sex toys, thinking that purchasing and using them meant that you or your partner alone wasn't enough?

5. Do you need alcohol or drugs to muster up enough confidence to enjoy uninhibited sex? (The sidebar in chapter 18 lists a few alternatives to explore.)

6. There's a common misconception that a woman's sex drive diminishes as she ages. I contend that it's not the sex drive, it's the adoration, enthusiasm, and skill of her partner that diminishes. Do you agree?

7. How has your age impacted your sex life? Write an essay just for you that tracks the way your sexual prowess, energy, and interest have changed as you've aged.

8. In your opinion, are you open enough about your sexuality?

9. Do you feel you have had enough "casual" sex? Write a letter to yourself about your conquests, or lack thereof, and your feelings about them. Without any judgment, reflect on the role casual sex did or did not play in your life journey.

Chapter 19: Religion

1. At any point in your life, did you question if your religion was enough of a pathway to living a spiritual life?

2. For you, is religion spiritual or cultural or both? Do you feel you have enough of a spiritual or religious presence in your life?

3. If you left the faith in which you were raised, when did you realize you no longer belonged there?

4. How much do you know about religions other than your own? Would you read about them or attend a service, in order to learn more? If you created your own religion, what would it look like?

5. Can you imagine a world without religion? What would it look and

feel like? If there were no religion, do you believe the world would be at peace?

6. Do you believe that most organized religions offer enough of an ethical template for every age and stage of life? What positive aspects of your character do you attribute to having grown up with, or without, organized religion?

7. Do you consider yourself religious enough? If yes, how does religion define you? If no, do you have another spiritual practice?

8. Who in your life incorporates enough spirituality to inspire your own personal growth? List your religious and/or spiritual role models. They need not be religious leaders. Write about the qualities you admire in each and the valuable life lessons you learned through their examples.

Chapter 20: Money

1. Do you believe there is such a thing as enough money?
2. Is it possible to be considered successful without great wealth?
3. How old were you when you first spent your own money?
4. This is not a trick question: Does money buy happiness?
5. If you won a big lottery jackpot, what would you do with the prize money?
6. What role does money play in your definition of success?
7. What career would you choose (or have chosen) if you were independently wealthy?
8. Did you receive enough financial education? Who was your guide?
9. Is loving what you do as, or more important than, the money you earn?
10. Does the idea of retirement scare or excite you? List the pros and cons.
11. Who is the most successful person you know? What, in your opinion, makes them successful?
12. What life decisions would you have made differently if money was of no consequence? How has your answer changed over your lifetime?

13. Aside from material possessions, in your opinion, what does money buy? What has money (any amount) meant to you and your family? Write about a time where it turned out that money was not the problem solver you thought it would be.

Chapter 21: Time

1. Do you consider yourself a patient enough person in all aspects of your life? If not, what tests your patience most?
2. Can you recall a moment in your life that overwhelmed you with a sense of gratitude?
3. Can you identify a moment in time that inspired your professional or personal pursuits?
4. How do you measure time? By birthdays? The calendar year? Or . . .
5. What must you do in order to feel you haven't wasted the day? Do you consider relaxation wasteful, or can it be purposeful?
6. Are you able to make enough time for people who are important to you?
7. What's your most vivid example of the passing of time?
8. If you were able to travel back in time, where would you go and when would it be?
9. Do you consider boredom time wasted, or time for relaxation? When was the last time you let yourself get bored enough to daydream? (A few benefits of boredom are listed in the sidebar in chapter 21.)
10. What are your favorite time management tools?
11. Since there are more than enough premade foods at the market and food delivery is so easy, do you consider cooking from scratch a waste of time?
12. Think about how you schedule time with your family. List your favorite shared rituals and routines. List ways you would like to restructure your family time. Would your family members welcome these ideas? If not, how do you think your family would like to spend time together?

13. Think about how you schedule time for yourself. List your favorite solo rituals and activities. Are you content with your work/family/self balance? If you had two hours every day to do whatever you like, how would you spend them?

14. The late Rose Fitzgerald Kennedy was quoted as saying, "It has been said that time heals all wounds. I don't agree." What do you think?

Chapter 22: Life

1. Do you feel as if you have truly lived enough of your life on your own terms?

2. Whose life do you admire most and why?

3. How might you give your loved ones enough information to keep your memory alive for generations to come? (See the sidebar in chapter 22 for my ideas.)

4. Has your life turned out as you imagined it would be? What was the biggest surprise?

5. Have you left anything unsaid to your loved ones with the assumption that you have enough time to do so?

6. Do you have any nagging regrets? Write them down and rank them in order of possibility for resolution. Then write out a plan of attack to shorten your list of regrets.

7. I have no idea what "acting my age" means. How do you define it? Please join my Facebook group at https://facebook.com/howmuch-isenoughbook and share your thoughts.

8. If you had the opportunity to live your life over again, would you do anything differently? The answer to this question can be a huge gift from you to you. Think of it as a future mission statement, understanding that there is still time in your life to make important changes. If you have children, consider sharing this answer with them.

ACKNOWLEDGMENTS

I will never be able to thank these wonderful, insightful people enough for their valuable contributions and support. Thank you to my team at DartFrog Publishing—Gordon McClellan, Amy Bachelder, Suanne Laqueur, Chris Dorning, Mark Hobbs, Lee Cart, Simona Meloni and Sarah Treppiedi. I would also like to thank Yeonwoo Biak, Sam Berger, Gary Donzig, Nancy Giles, Scott Ginsberg, Galia Gichon, Alvin and Natalie Goldstein, Bob Goldstein, Wendy Hammers, and the beautiful tribe of writers at Kick Back & Create, Jennifer Heitler, Paula Holt, Peggy Klaus, Michelle La Pierre, Jenna, Patrick, Natalie, and Adrienne Landi, Jill Leiderman, Frankie Miller, Kathy O'Malley, Andrea Rawitt, Nancy Rawlinson, and my insightful classmates at The Sackett Street Writers Workshop, Gilbert Sare, Jill Sare, Louise Stahl, Jeff and Marla Vaughn, Jane Voigts, Susan Yeagley, and Betsy Zeger.

ABOUT THE AUTHOR

Claire Berger began writing, *How Much Is Enough,* her interactive memoir, to tap into the ever-present conversation buzzing around in our heads: *How much is enough . . . Exercise? Religion? Shoes? Family? Food? Sex?* Claire tackles an extensive array of topics in twenty-two thought-provoking chapters, to be read in no particular order. For over four decades, Claire Berger has been earning a living as a comedian, improv performer, and writer while simultaneously embracing her all-time favorite job, being mom to her daughter Jenna and son Sam and LaLa to her granddaughters Natalie and Adrienne.

For more information, visit www.claireberger.com